HOPE THAT NEVER FAILS

ALSO BY JOSEPH PRINCE

Give Me This Mountain

Unstoppable Faith

Eat Your Way to Life and Health

No More Mind Games

Anchored

Live the Let-Go Life

The Prayer of Protection

Grace Revolution

The Power of Right Believing

Unmerited Favor

Destined to Reign

Healing Promises

Provision Promises

Health and Wholeness Through the Holy Communion

For more information on these books and other inspiring resources, visit JosephPrince.com.

JOSEPH PRINCE

HOPE THAT NEVER FAILS

LIVE CONFIDENT IN TROUBLING TIMES

All bold in Scripture quotations were added by the author for emphasis.

Hope That Never Fails—Live Confident in Troubling Times

ISBN 978-981-14-8713-2

Joseph Prince Resources
JosephPrince.com

Printed in the Republic of Singapore
First edition

CONTENTS

INTRODUCTION

In the times we live in today, with virulent diseases, economic uncertainty, and all sorts of dangers being part of our daily lives, is it still possible to wake up every morning with a strong sense of hope?

Without a shadow of doubt, our Lord's answer to this question is a resounding **yes**!

The Bible calls God **the God of hope** (Rom. 15:13). And it's precisely in the midst of dark times that He wants us to remember He **is** the God of hope, and He wants to fill us with so much joy and peace that we don't simply **have** hope, but can even **overflow with hope**.

I'm not talking about the kind of hope the world offers that is uncertain and has no power to bring about the miracle you need. This hope that God wants you to be overflowing with is a strong, certain, and powerful hope. A hope that is always sure, that does not disappoint and does not put you to shame (Rom. 5:5). A hope that never fails.

Really? you might be thinking. *Is there even such a thing—a hope that never disappoints?*

Yes, my friend. That is exactly what Bible hope is. Unlike the hope of the world, it isn't based on optimism or wishful thinking. Our hope is anchored on the promises of God and our God cannot lie (Heb. 6:18). Our hope is based on all that our Lord Jesus has done for us. Because of His finished work at Calvary, we can come boldly to His throne of grace and find grace to help us in our time of need (Heb. 4:16).

I'm not saying that everything you pray for will happen immediately or that you will not go through any challenges. We live in a fallen world, and the fact is, you and I will face trials and tribulation (John 16:33). But even when if it seems like there is no way out of your predicament and all your prayers have seemingly gone unanswered, I want to personally encourage you to believe that **you can still have hope**—because our Lord Jesus is on **your** side (Rom. 8:31).

Will you take up His invitation for you to trust Him, to rest in Him, and to hope again?

Maybe you're facing a situation right now that looks hopeless. It may be a weakness or addiction you've tried again and again to overcome and you are at the brink of giving up. Perhaps you have been praying for healing from a disease but every prognosis you have received has only put more fear in your heart. Maybe it feels like you are slowly being crushed by mounting debts. No matter how much you try, your outstanding amounts only seem to compound and increase. Or perhaps you have been searching for a life partner but after going on date after date with no results, you can't bring yourself to try again.

Beloved, it's no coincidence that you are holding this book right at this time.

I believe the Lord is reaching out to you. He understands your struggles. He sees the challenges others may not see, the disappointments no one else knows about. And He wants you to know that you are not alone—you have a Savior who loves you deeply, favors you highly, and has nothing but good plans for your life. The One with whom all things are possible is saying to you, "Don't give up. It's not over. Because I love you, I will protect and deliver you. I will heal your body. And I will restore double for all your troubles (Zech. 9:12). Keep trusting Me—your breakthrough is coming!"

I know it is not easy to hold on to hope when circumstances are screaming at you to give up. It's not easy to keep believing that His promises are true when you have prayed, trusted, and prayed again . . . and still not see results. Perhaps, like the psalmist, you have been crying out, "How long, O LORD? Will You forget me forever? How long will You hide Your face from me?" (Ps. 13:1).

That's why I've put together this book for you based on eight powerful messages I have preached that I believe will impart strong, Bible hope into your heart. If you need fresh hope today for your situation, get ready to receive it because His Word tells us that it is "through the encouragement of the Scriptures we might have hope" (Rom. 15:4 ESV).

If you are going through a night season in your life right now, I believe you will find the encouragement and strength you need in the message, *God of the Valleys*. May you catch a revelation of how our Lord Jesus is right there with you in your lowest moments. Even when you're too tired to even pray, He is there with you. I pray that you'll learn how He is your Door of Hope in the valley of trouble and how you can rest in the victory He has won for you.

Perhaps you're anxious about how you and your loved ones can get through these dark times safely protected against not just physical dangers but also the perilous pestilences and financial famine plaguing the world today. I wrote *Specially Protected to Live Unafraid* to help you immerse yourself in His promises of protection for you and your family. As you allow me to show you the riches hidden in Psalm 91, may you begin to live unafraid and experience a new level of protection and well-being.

Even if the enemy has stolen from you—from your health, your relationships, or your finances—all is not lost. You have a God of restoration! And if you have believed the lie that you have no right to ask the Lord for help because the trouble you are in is a result of your own mistakes or if you have been living in crushing regret because you feel you have wasted years of your life, I want to encourage you to take some time to read *Expect to Receive God's Much-More Restoration.* I believe the Lord has given me a message for you that will impart hope to you and give you a fresh revelation of just how good He is.

These are just a few of the messages in this book that I know the Lord wants your heart anchored in, especially if you're feeling discouraged or fighting depressive thoughts today. It is my prayer that as you feed on these messages, you will find the strength to hold on to His promises for you and to **hope**, even when in the natural, it looks like there is no reason to (Rom. 4:18 NLT). Your breakthrough may not come immediately but I believe that your negative situation **will** turn around. Even if all you see are small improvements, take heart and trust that your 30-fold breakthrough will become 60-fold and finally, a 100-fold harvest. Hope afresh in His love for you because it will not disappoint—your healing, provision, deliverance, and restoration are all on their way!

1.
HOPE THAT DOESN'T DISAPPOINT

I hope I get the job. I really need it.

I hope our daughter knows how much we love her and stops hanging with the wrong crowd.

I really hope this infection gets nipped in the bud quickly and not get worse.

As a pastor, I've encountered many people, including believers, who've expressed their personal hopes, just like these, but all the while deeply uncertain that any of those hopes would come to pass. Oftentimes, their expressions of hope are laced with discouragement and concern that the very opposite may happen instead.

Maybe this has happened to you. Maybe you've even fervently said, "*I hope so*," when you and your lunch buddies were talking about whether a good bonus was coming at the end of the year, but deep inside, you were actually more certain you wouldn't get it.

How can we have a hope that is not left to chance or the forces out there, or to the whims and fancies of fickle and imperfect human beings? How can we have a hope that is not affected by the mistakes we have accumulated or dependent on our limited knowledge and abilities?

My friend, I want to introduce you to what I call "Bible hope"—the kind of hope that does not disappoint or play you out. A hope that translates into a positive expectation of good, fortifying and energizing your heart. Why is it so sure and certain? Because it's anchored to something immovable, unshakable, and utterly trustworthy—the love of Christ and His finished work at Calvary.

WHEN YOU HOPE IN CHRIST AND IN HIS LOVE FOR YOU, THAT HOPE WILL NOT DISAPPOINT!

If you want to live life with this confident expectation of good and see the good you're hoping for come to pass, then I pray you get this deep inside you today: Nothing can ever separate you from the love of our Lord Jesus. Nothing can ever undo His finished work. If there's one man you can trust a hundred percent all of the time, someone who will never fail you, it's Christ Jesus. When you hope in Him and His love for you, that hope will not disappoint!

A MOTHER'S HOPE REALIZED

Anita, a single mother living in Virginia, United States, with her two teenaged kids, shared a testimony with me about having exactly this hope alight in her, giving her strength throughout her wait for her breakthrough.

Laid off from her position as a production supervisor in a manufacturing plant, Anita faced the very real possibility of financial strain in paying household bills on time and putting food on the table unless a decent-paying job came her way. Refusing to entertain fears and negative thoughts during her period of unemployment, Anita chose instead to look to the Lord, His love, and His wonderful promises for her found in His Word. She kept her focus on His grace as she listened to my sermons non-stop, playing them even while she was asleep!

Full of the Lord's love for her, she prayed and asked Him for her dream job—a position as a human resource manager. She told me how, in the months that came and went as she waited for employment, a deep abiding assurance and confidence guarded her heart. Her hope in the Lord to provide what she and her family needed was so strong that when people asked, she just told them with unshakable certainty that everything was going to be fine.

What kept such a hope alive in her and what did it result in? I'll let Anita tell you in her own words:

> *As I listened to the sermons, the love of my heavenly Father and Jesus became so true in my heart that I just knew everything was going to be fine. Whenever the bills were due, I would hear the Lord tell me, "Take no thought for tomorrow, My grace is sufficient for you." Sure enough, everything always worked out fine.*
>
> *After ten months, the chief executive officer of an organization gave me a call. She told me that she was looking through the former human resource manager's desk and came across my résumé, and just had a desire to interview me. At the interview, she hired me on the spot! When I told her my salary expectations, she responded by saying that she was going to give me significantly more than*

what I wanted. Praise the Lord. I am now employed in my dream job and I know the Lord sent me here. It's just wonderful!

What an encouraging testimony! The steadfast hope that Anita experienced guarded her heart against paralyzing fears and anxiety during the period she was unemployed. Her hope was unshakable only because she knew how much the Lord loved her. And she wasn't disappointed. The Lord never failed to provide for her family's needs when they arose. And not only did He answer her prayer and give her her dream job, but He also gave her a higher-than-expected salary!

HOPE ANCHORED TO GOD'S LOVE

My friend, this is the kind of hope that I want you to have. Bible hope is a strong, joyful, and confident expectation of good happening to you that is based on the unchanging Word of God and not the changing words of man. It is anchored to the perfect love of our Lord and not to the imperfect love or ability of man. And it has, as its solid, unshakable foundation, the finished work of Christ.

This is why Romans 5:5 says, "Now hope does not disappoint, because the love of God has been poured out in our hearts by the Holy Spirit who was given to us." **His love** is what guarantees our hope. The reason you and I can "know so" rather than just "hope so" that good things will happen to us is that God loves us! And He demonstrated this love at the cross when He gave up His own Son to die for our sins. Now, if He spared not His Son, how will He not with Him also freely give us all things (Rom. 8:32)?

Beloved, God does not want you to go through the storms of life with a wishy-washy, I sure-hope-so-but-I'm-*so*-not-sure attitude, tossed to and fro by uncertainties, anxieties, and fears. No, He loves you so much He wants your soul stable and anchored with know-so Bible hope—a confident, positive expectation of good from Him who doesn't disappoint. He wants you to enjoy sure, steadfast hope that carries you through every trial to amazing breakthroughs and victories.

So I want to encourage you today to hope in the Lord, His love, and what He has done for you through the cross. If you are facing some financial trouble, I want you to go from saying, "*Things are bad and I'm just hoping I'll pull through*" to saying, "I am confident the situation will turn around and I will be abundantly supplied because Jesus loves me!" Bible hope will give you the confidence to believe and say this.

YOU CAN LIVE EACH DAY WITH A CONFIDENT EXPECTATION OF GOOD HAPPENING TO YOU BECAUSE YOU HAVE A HEAVENLY FATHER WHO WATCHES OVER YOU CAREFULLY, LOVES YOU DEEPLY, FAVORS YOU HIGHLY, AND HAS NOTHING BUT GOOD PLANS FOR YOUR LIFE!

My friend, you can live each day with a confident expectation of good happening to you because you are not like the people of the world—you are a child of the Most High God. You have a heavenly Father who watches over you carefully, loves you deeply, favors you highly, and has nothing but good plans for your life!

HOPE, THE FUEL OF FAITH

You may be thinking, *"Why is it so important to have Bible hope? What's the big deal?"*

My friend, Bible hope is important because it is a crucial ingredient for faith. Without hope, your faith cannot work. Hebrews 11:1 says, "Now faith is the substance of things hoped for, the evidence of things not seen." If you don't have hope, how can you have faith? If you don't have a confident expectation of good, what is there to give substance to your faith? So having hope is necessary and important, because it fuels your faith.

Consider the woman with the issue of blood in the Bible. For twelve years, she had a chronic bleeding condition. She spent all her money seeking treatment from various physicians, but none of the treatments helped her. In fact, the Bible tells us that she "had suffered many things from many physicians . . . and was no better, but rather grew worse" (Mark 5:26).

Most women would have given up on ever being cured, but this poor woman didn't. She began to have Bible hope when she heard about the loving Savior. Let's follow the story in Mark 5:27–29:

> When she heard about Jesus, she came behind Him in the crowd and touched His garment. For she said, "If only I may touch His clothes, I shall be made well." Immediately the fountain of her blood was dried up, and she felt in her body that she was healed of the affliction.

Do you see? Because of what she had heard about Jesus, a confident expectation of receiving good from Jesus arose on the inside of her and ignited her faith to believe that if she could just touch His clothes, she would be made whole.

What caused this woman to brave the crowds, whom she knew could rightfully stone her for being in public in her unclean condition, and draw near to Jesus and take her healing from Him? It was bold faith fueled by Bible hope. And this hope didn't disappoint because it was based on Jesus' love. The more she heard about how Jesus willingly healed the diseased and despised—people like her—the more she began to see not a God of judgment but a God of love and compassion, and the more hope and unconscious faith grew in her.

IF YOU ARE BELIEVING GOD FOR HEALING TODAY, DON'T FOCUS ON WHETHER YOU HAVE "SUFFICIENT" FAITH OR NOT. JUST KEEP HEARING ABOUT JESUS—HIS LOVE, HIS GRACE, AND HIS GOODNESS TOWARD YOU

Beloved, if you are believing God for healing in your body today, don't focus on whether you have "sufficient" faith or not (there is no record in the Bible that the woman did this). Just keep hearing about Jesus—His love, His grace, and His goodness toward you. See from the Gospels how He healed the sick without any strings attached. Never once did He condemn anyone for being sick or chide anyone for daring to ask Him for healing. He willingly healed **all** who came to Him, no matter what their histories were. As you hear about His goodness and have a personal revelation of His love for you, a confident, positive expectation of good from the Lord will arise in your heart. Firmly established upon His love, this hope will fuel your faith so that like the woman with the issue of blood, you will reach out boldly to receive your miracle!

THE MISSING LINK

Allow me to share with you another testimony on the power of Bible hope. Alice and her husband, a precious couple from Pennsylvania, US, wanted a child of their own. They tried for ten years, but Alice just could not conceive. She had even undergone a year of fertility treatments, only to develop a large, painful cyst on her right ovary. The cyst was removed through a laparoscopy, but after the surgery, she was diagnosed with severe endometriosis. Despite this turn of events, Alice chose to believe God would bless her with a child, regardless of the odds against her.

Months passed and Alice still did not conceive. Then one day, she heard a sermon of mine that explained Bible hope and encouraged her to hope in a gracious God. She also learned that this God had made her righteous and qualified her for every blessing through Jesus' sacrifice on the cross. With Bible hope in her heart birthed out of a fresh revelation of God's love for her, Alice told God that she wanted a champion of a baby. To God be the glory, Alice conceived not long after. And after a supernaturally easy pregnancy and labor, she and her husband now have a beautiful baby boy named Noah!

"I was told that people with the level of endometriosis I was diagnosed with only have a one to two percent chance of conceiving without treatment and that even with in vitro fertilization, the chances are low," she said. "Yet, here is Noah—by the grace of God!"

When did her turning point come? Let me share with you what Alice explained so poignantly:

> *As I listened to your message, I realized how I had focused so much on trying to have faith for a baby, but was really afraid to hope for a baby in the "positive expectation of good" way you described. I'd thought that daring to hope would bring me more disappointment because I'd never heard that hope was a sure thing for those in Christ. This was the missing link for me in understanding faith as the substance of things hoped for, not a work or level of belief I needed to maintain.*

Isn't that beautiful? Hope sprang up in her heart when she realized that faith is not something that she had to work at or try to maintain. And when she realized that hope "was a sure thing for those in Christ," her faith just skyrocketed. This is why the Bible says faith is the substance of things **hoped** for. Your faith can't take you where you want to go without the fuel of hope. And, as Alice discovered, this hope is a **sure thing**, an unshakable expectation of a most favorable outcome. It is my prayer that you will, like Alice, learn to grow in and always have a positive expectation of good, knowing that God loves you and wants to fulfill the deepest desires of your heart.

Beloved, if you are sick right now, I want to encourage you to keep on having a confident expectation that you will get better. If you lack financially, keep on having a positive expectation that supply is on the way. Keep on hoping that that wayward teenager will become a man or woman of God. Keep on hoping, knowing that this hope will not disappoint because it is anchored to the Lord's love and finished work. And one of these days, sooner than you think, you will relish the fruit of your hope!

KEEP YOUR HOPES UP BY HEARING

How do you keep your hopes up as you wait patiently for the manifestation of your blessing? You simply keep hearing about the goodness and faithfulness of the Lord!

Beloved, as you continue to hope in the Lord for your miracle, just keep hearing messages that are full of His love and grace toward you, and how much He wants to meet your need. Fill yourself with new covenant promises found in His Word and keep your focus on His unmerited favor. Know that it's not about what you have to do, but all about what He has done at the cross to secure your blessing. Constantly hearing about God's goodness and faithfulness was what made all the difference for Alice. She shared:

> *I listened to your messages over and over again as they encouraged me to focus on Christ and God's promises instead of my symptoms. In one of the messages, I heard you say, "God is faithful," several times in a row. Each time you said it, I felt hope rise up in my spirit.*
>
> *My head was saying, "It's been so many years. Give up and spare yourself this torture of waiting for something that will never happen." But when I heard you say "God is faithful" repeatedly with such authority, those voices in my head would pale in the*

light of that hope. I believe the Holy Spirit guided you to say that in just the right number of times for me to get it deep down into my spirit!

Can you see how hearing and hearing about the Lord's love and promises for you imparts hope? God wants you to abound in hope (Rom. 15:13). And as in Alice's case, constantly listening to good news about Jesus is how you abound in hope, silence the negative voices, and protect your mind. Apostle Paul told the believers in Thessalonica to put on as a helmet, the **hope** of salvation (1 Thess. 5:8). Hope that you will be saved from whatever you need God to save you from is the spiritual armor that protects your mind and keeps you going!

BIBLE HOPE SPEAKS AND SEES

How else does Bible hope grow in your heart? Well, by you speaking hope-filled words. Hebrews 10:23 says, "Let us hold fast the confession of our hope without wavering, for He who promised is faithful." The more your words are seasoned with Bible hope based on God's steadfast promises and faithfulness, the closer you are to the manifestation of your blessing.

When you wake up in the morning, instead of saying, *"Oh man, it's going to be a dreadful day,"* remind yourself of the Lord's love for you and say, "Lord Jesus, I know this will be a great day simply because You love me. Your perfect love surrounds me and drives out all fear. Your favor is all over me to open doors that are good for me. It's going to be a beautiful day filled with Your goodness!"

At the same time, learn to develop positive mental pictures that are prompted by God's promises. Our human tendency is to imagine the worst-case scenarios. So if you are sick and lying in bed, picture yourself strong and full of life, doing your favorite activity. See yourself running in the park with your children, or enjoying a hearty meal with your friends. Say, "Lord, because Your stripes have purchased healing for me (Isa. 53:5), I cannot but get well!" If you are believing God for a child, picture yourself cuddling that baby. See yourself making funny faces at your bundle of joy as you change his diapers! Tell the Lord, "Because children are a gift from You (Ps. 127:3), I will bring forth a champion who will be a delight to my soul and who will do mighty things for Your kingdom!"

YOU HAVE EVERY REASON TO HOPE

My friend, unlike the people of the world, you have every reason to hope even when the odds are stacked against you because you are standing on favor ground. Because of our Lord Jesus' sacrifice for you, you are now God's beloved child. You are totally justified, accepted, and qualified by Jesus' blood. You are forever highly favored in Christ the Beloved. God is on your side and He is for your success in all aspects of life!

You can be like Abraham, who "contrary to hope, in hope believed, so that he became the father of many nations" (Rom. 4:18). Abraham faced an impossible situation. At about a century old, what were his chances of fathering a child? And his aged wife, Sarah, was by now doubly barren since she was already barren when she was much younger (Rom. 4:19). Imagine also all the gossip and jokes the couple had to endure, especially when God changed Abram's name to *Abraham*, meaning "father of a multitude,"[1] when they didn't even have a single child to show for it!

BECAUSE OF OUR LORD JESUS' SACRIFICE FOR YOU, YOU ARE FOREVER HIGHLY FAVORED IN CHRIST. GOD IS ON YOUR SIDE AND HE IS FOR YOUR SUCCESS IN ALL ASPECTS OF LIFE!

Yet, despite all this, Abraham remained hopeful, knowing his hope was not in his own ability to father a child, but in his trustworthy, unchangeable God, whose love and promises never fail. The result? God gave them a beautiful miracle baby whom they named Isaac, and through Isaac, Abraham indeed "became the father of many nations."

So let me encourage you to keep on hoping despite the odds because like Abraham and Sarah, you have a God of impossibilities who loves you and who cannot fail. It doesn't matter what the reports say or what the statistics show. When you have Bible hope that is firmly anchored to God's love, it is only a matter of time before your miracle manifests.

I love how Alice wrapped up her testimony of receiving the baby she believed God for. This is what she said:

> *Our God is not a God of statistical probability. He is a sure hope and with Him, all things are possible. I had two different doctors during my pregnancy. Both of them asked with amazement how*

I'd conceived after they reviewed my history and failed attempts with fertility treatments. I just replied, "By the grace of God!"

God is just in delivering on every promise because Jesus has made us one hundred percent eligible, and He doesn't ask us to make excuses for Him! Rather, He asks us to hold Him to His promise as Abraham did, believing that "what He had promised, He was also able to perform." We must know that every good promise in God's Word was written for us.

I just love that—**God is not a God of statistical probability, but a sure hope with whom all things are possible**. Beloved, this is your God! This is why you can hope against all hope and not have that hope disappoint. This is why you can live life with a confident and joyful expectation that good things will happen to you because the Lord loves you!

2.

GOD OF THE VALLEYS

Two little flocks of goats.

That's how the Bible described the Israelite army in 1 Kings 20. And what were they up against? A vastly superior Syrian force complete with captains, horses, and chariots that filled the countryside.

Totally surrounded. Overwhelmingly outnumbered.

For seven days the two armies camped opposite each other. For seven long days, God's people had no shortage of opportunities to see how small and vulnerable they were against their enemies.

Day by day the tension must have mounted in the Israeli camp: *If God was going to fight for us as He'd said He would, why didn't He do it already?*

Just imagine the anxiety and despair that must have gripped their hearts. Possibly, thoughts of surrender may have plagued their minds. *What madness is this? How can our little army have any chance against the marauding hordes of Syrians out for vengeance? Surely we will be crushed!*

Now, this wasn't the first time the two armies were facing off.

They had fought the year before, and the Lord had caused the small Israelite army to thrash their enemies. The Syrians, stung by that defeat, amassed a great army to once again attack the Israelites. And this time, they strategized their attack at a place they believed the Israelites would be vulnerable.

This time round, the Syrians were supremely confident as the king's advisers had said, "Their gods are gods of the hills. Therefore they were stronger than we; but if we fight against them in the plain, surely we will be stronger than they" (1 Kings 20:23).

GOD OF THE MOUNTAINS AND THE VALLEYS

What the Syrians were really saying is that the God of Israel would only help His people when they were up in the mountains; He wouldn't be with them when they were down in the valley.

Today, some Christians believe this myth too. They think God is a "mountaintop God"—that He only helps them when they haven't made mistakes, when they are impeccably holy and full of faith. They believe that He invites them up to where He is when they are doing everything right, but leaves them to fend for themselves when they mess up or are discouraged and in despair.

My friend, if that is you, I'm here to declare to you that our Lord is God of the mountain and He is also God of the valley. Certainly, He is with you on the mountaintop—when you see His victory and His glory and when you are in your high moments. But He's also with you in your low moments to help you just like He did for the Israelites in 1 Kings 20.

How do I know? Because that's exactly what He told the Israelites who were facing the Syrian horde: "Because the Syrians have said, 'The LORD is God of the hills, but He is not God of the valleys,' therefore I will deliver all this great multitude into your hand, and you shall know that I am the LORD" (1 Kings 20:28).

THE LORD IS WITH YOU IN YOUR HIGH MOMENTS. BUT HE'S ALSO WITH YOU IN YOUR LOW MOMENTS—WHEN YOU ARE IN THE VALLEY—TO HELP YOU.

And on the seventh day, the battle finally broke out and the children of Israel killed one hundred thousand Syrian foot soldiers. The rest of the enemy fled to a nearby city where the Lord caused a wall to fall on another twenty-seven thousand of the men who were left.

Imagine that! An army said to be the size of two little flocks of goats defeating one hundred thousand enemy soldiers in a day. Isn't that just amazing? The Lord delivered the Israelites and gave them a resounding victory! Undisputedly, He showed Himself as God of the valley.

HE IS WITH YOU TO DELIVER YOU

Maybe you are having a valley moment right now. Perhaps you're stuck in a valley called sickness, depression, or debt and you can't see a way out. Your challenge seems so huge and your strength to tackle the enormity of your circumstances feels like two tiny flocks of goats against a marauding army filling the countryside. And you're wondering . . .

Am I going to stay in this valley forever? How can I ever get out? Where is God in my situation? He said He would deliver me, but where is He? Has He left me all by myself?

Beloved, whatever valley you find yourself in today, I want to encourage you with this truth: as you walk through your darkest valley, Jesus, the Lord of the mountaintops, the Lord who is mighty to save, is right there with you right NOW. He has not left you nor abandoned you.

AS YOU WALK THROUGH YOUR DARKEST VALLEY, JESUS, THE LORD WHO IS MIGHTY TO SAVE, IS RIGHT THERE WITH YOU.

No matter how deep your valley of trouble might seem, like David, you can believe and say Psalm 23:4: "Yea, though I walk through the valley of the shadow of death, I will fear no evil; for You are with me; Your rod and Your staff, they comfort me."

Notice the personal pronoun "You" used in this verse? The Lord showed me that when we're going through a trial, it's no longer enough to just talk **about** Him as David was doing in the earlier verses—"The Lord is my shepherd . . . He makes me lie down . . . He leads me by the still waters." When we are in the valley, we need to see Him personally with us and talk **to** Him **directly**.

That's what David was doing. In the same way, when you're facing a trial, say to the Lord, "You are with me. Your rod and Your staff are protecting and defending me. I will fear no evil for You are with me. You prepare a table before me. You anoint my head with oil" (Ps. 23:4–5).

Do you know what can result from this?

Psalm 23:6 tells us, "Surely goodness and mercy shall follow me all the days of my life; and I will dwell in the house of the LORD forever."

Surely goodness and mercy shall follow you! Do you see that? In Hebrew, it actually says God's goodness and mercy "**will hunt you down**!"[1] You can't run fast enough to evade His goodness and mercy! As you practice His presence when fears and discouragement swamp your heart, not only will it change your perspective to see that God's goodness is on your side, but you will also see that very goodness hunting you down!

DOUBLE FOR YOUR TROUBLE

Child of the Most High God, no matter how dark your valley looks right now, His Word promises that you are not going to be stuck there forever. The enemy wants you to believe you're all alone in your struggle but that's a lie. You are not alone and helpless. Like David, you are the Lord's beloved! He is with you to be your very present help in time of trouble (Ps. 46:1), and more than anyone else, He knows what you're going through.

And just as the Lord was with David to give him victory over

Goliath in the valley of Elah and to deliver him when he was hiding from Saul in the wilderness, the Lord will give you your breakthrough because He loves you. You are going to walk through the valley and emerge victorious because the Lord IS with you!

But Pastor Prince, you don't understand. The trouble I am in is hopeless. I can't see any way out. I can't beat the odds.

If you find yourself in a place where your hopes have been crushed and you're battling nothing but dark, depressive thoughts with no sight of light, I have great encouragement for you from the Lord in Zechariah 9:12:

> Return to the stronghold, you prisoners of hope. Even today I declare that I will restore double to you.

The Lord calls you a prisoner of hope because double restoration is on its way to you!

YOU DON'T HAVE TO LIVE IN DEFEAT —THE LORD'S POWERFUL RESTORATION IS ON THE WAY!

Beloved, I don't know what valley you are in right now. Maybe the doctors have just given you a bad report. Perhaps you're broke and facing a mountain of debts. Maybe your marriage is crumbling and looks irreparable. However bad it seems, it's not over because you have a loving Savior who is willing and able to turn things around for you. You don't have to live in defeat—the Lord's powerful restoration is on the way!

RESTORATION AND BEAUTY FOR ASHES

My ministry office has received many testimonies from people who have experienced such restoration over the years. Here, I want to share with you one such testimony from Iris of Oregon in the United States to show you how good the Lord truly is and why you can trust His Word of restoration for you even if your situation appears hopeless and bleak.

Iris had written in to share how she had to grapple with serious troubles in her previous marriage. She was married for almost a decade to a man who had changed over the years and became a different person because of his drug addiction. To feed his drug habit, he got himself into bad company and his association with them made Iris feel unsafe even in their own home. She soon began to face depression and anxiety issues and had to be on anti-depressants. As she recalled that low point in her life, she said:

> *During those dark days, I clung to the Lord and found in Him everything I needed. I also listened to Pastor Prince's messages on how Jesus is our door of hope in our valley of trouble, and was so encouraged. Even though I had moments of extreme doubt, the Lord still held me close in His embrace. It was His presence that strengthened me and gave me peace to the point I didn't need the anti-depressant medication anymore.*
>
> *Eventually, my husband left the house and left me in the lurch when some of the people in his drug circle threatened to harm us. Even though he came back later when the situation improved, he*

continued with his drug use—that was all that mattered to him. Our marriage eventually broke down and ended.

But God is a God of restoration! He enabled me to go to church, find a new job and even a new home. He has also blessed me with a new husband who loves me dearly. Friends and family say this man is so well suited to me that it must be God—even my husband agrees with this! The Lord has truly given me beauty for ashes and now, I'm living the abundant life!

I want to encourage those who are going through trials in life to trust our Daddy God and Lord Jesus, our wonderful Savior. Thank you, Pastor Prince, for pointing me to my door of hope when I was in the valley of trouble!

I was personally so encouraged to read Iris's testimony! I can only imagine how frightening and lonely some of those days were for her, and I'm so glad she found ways to keep hearing about the Lord's love for her and allowing that word to strengthen her heart and faith. And what a powerful work of restoration the Lord brought into Iris's life! I loved reading how the Lord took care of all her needs—physical, emotional, and material—and restored to her all that she had lost. My friend, He is waiting to do the same for you too.

Our Lord is a wonderful Savior. He is not just a God of the mountain, but He is also a God of the valley who restores! When you feel yourself spiraling into despair with no ability to expect good things to ever happen to you, take time to plug in and listen to messages about Jesus' love for you. They will restore you to being a prisoner of hope and start you on your journey of receiving your restoration.

YOUR DOOR OF HOPE IN THE VALLEY

Like the Israelites in 1 Kings 20, you could be facing one attack after another, experiencing one trouble after another. You could have tried every way you know of to climb out but all you see is darkness and you can't find a way out. If that is you, I want to remind you of a beautiful verse in Hosea 2:15 that clearly reveals God's heart for you: "I will give her her vineyards from there, and the Valley of Achor as a door of hope."

In Hebrew, *Achor* means "trouble."[2] What the Lord is saying to you is this: "In your valley of trouble, I will open a door of hope for you."

What a glorious promise! Notice that this door of hope is not found on the mountaintop. The Lord knows we will have times of trial and seasons of darkness. That is why He has promised and put a door of hope in our valleys. That is why we may find ourselves going through a valley but we will not stay there. We will go through it and come out the other side.

The enemy may whisper in your mind, *"Oh no, you're here to stay in this valley. Your situation is beyond hope."* My friend, that's the time to look for the door of hope. And you open that door simply by having a confident, positive expectation of good from the Lord who loves you. You'll step through that door of hope as Iris did simply by knowing that He is with you, holding you and carrying you through this trial.

Don't allow pessimistic thoughts about your situation and the talk of naysayers to weigh you down. Even if it looks like the situation is beyond saving, hear the words of your loving Savior to you: "Don't be afraid. Only believe" (Mark 5:36). Only believe and rest in His perfect love for you. Put on the helmet of salvation—the helmet of hope in His goodness—and you will see your marriage and your children turn out well. You will begin to see bondages breaking, depression fleeing, and good things coming your way.

The world may say, *"I dare not raise my hopes too high."* But you are different because you are the Lord's beloved and He says to you, "Raise your hopes as high as the throne of God! Yes, these things are against you but with Me, you can hope and expect all things to work out for your good!"

BECAUSE HE PAID THE PRICE

Why can we expect to see God's love and goodness work on our behalf when we are in the valley? Because our Lord Jesus fully paid the price for it. And it was in a valley that it happened—at the foot of the Mount of Olives, in a garden called Gethsemane.

It was in that garden that the very thought of becoming sin on the cross brought on such extreme agony to our Lord, it caused Him to sweat droplets of blood that fell to the ground (Luke 22:44 NLT). In those long, soul-shattering moments, He was bearing your agony, your despair, and your depression upon Himself. He suffered terrible agony so that you would not have to be crushed by the terrible weight of stress, fear, and anxiety. The moment His blood—the sinless blood of God that redeems—combined with His sweat, He redeemed and bought you all out of hopelessness, anxiety attacks, depression, and all kinds of mental bondage.

But that's not all, my friend. His blood that fell to the ground has also reversed the curse on the ground (as a result of Adam's sin) for you so that you can continually walk in God's blessings and experience restoration for every trouble you are facing.

This is why you can raise your hopes even when the darkness in the valley threatens to engulf you—because the price has been paid and He is faithful to deliver to you all the blessings that He suffered and died to give you.

HE WILL TURN YOUR SITUATION AROUND

Many people ask, "*Why is this happening to me?*" when they find themselves in dark seasons. I don't have all the answers to your question but what I do know with certainty is this: The Lord is good. He loves you and He is never behind any pain you go through.

OUR LORD JESUS LOVES YOU AND HE IS NEVER BEHIND ANY PAIN YOU GO THROUGH. EVEN IF YOU HAVE NO STRENGTH TO CLING TO HIM, HE WILL HOLD YOUR HAND AND NEVER LET YOU GO.

The valley you are in right now may be full of troubles and seem hopeless like the Valley of Achor, but the Lord your deliverer is with you. Your shepherd, your shield, and the lifter of your head is with you (Ps. 3:3). He will never leave you nor forsake you and even if you have no strength to cling to Him, He will hold your hand and never let you go.

Right now, I'm reminded of a beautiful verse that I love from the New Century Version. It captures what the Lord has done for you so powerfully: "You protect me with your saving shield. You support me with your right hand. You have stooped to make me great" (Ps. 18:35).

He stooped.

Our Lord Jesus laid aside His crown of glory, laid aside His royal majesty, and came down all the way from heaven to earth, to the valley of our fallen human condition.

The altogether beautiful Jesus, who existed before Abram, who is the great I AM, stepped into a human body as a baby for the sole purpose of dying on the cross, to shed His precious blood, and to wash us clean from our sins so that He can bring us up to the Father's right hand.

Our King has stooped to crown us with His glory and honor and clothed us with His robes of righteousness. We are now His bride, sharing everything that He has, lacking nothing. That is the grace of our Lord.

He **stooped** so that without fear of disappointment, we can **raise our hopes high**—even in the darkest of valleys—and see them fulfilled because of His love and faithfulness.

My friend, our Lord Jesus is not just God of the mountain. When you do right, certainly, He is with you. But when you fail, all the more He is with you, holding you in His arms. He will never leave you; He will never forsake you. He's there in the valley with you to deliver you and lead you out. May your eyes be opened to see that the Lord IS your very present help in times of trouble. Now and forever, you are a prisoner of hope because the Lord will surely turn the situation around for you and restore to you double for your trouble!

3.

LAST TO FIRST WHEN YOU TRUST HIS GOODNESS

Do you often feel as if everyone around you is moving forward and doing promising or exciting stuff, while you're just left behind? Like when teams were picked in school and you were either not picked at all, or were the last one to be reluctantly called? It's as if nobody seems to want you on their team because you aren't strong enough, skillful enough, smart enough, good-looking enough, or cool enough.

If you've been living with these thoughts, God's got a word for you today.

The world may make you feel like you'll never amount to anything or that you'll always face rejection or limited success because of your weakness. But that's not how God sees you or your weakness. His ways are not the ways of the world, and I want to show you today how in His kingdom, the last is promoted to first. In His economy, the last and the least, the sidelined and the overlooked, are the ones who are chosen to receive His blessings in all their fullness.

The Bible is full of stories of heroes of faith who started out dismissed by others as being weak. Some were rejected even by their own families. Young David was one such character. Imagine how he must have felt when his father, Jesse, overlooked or conveniently forgot about him during prophet Samuel's visit to their home to anoint a new king for Israel. Jesse had eight sons including David, the youngest. But he only presented to Samuel the seven older brothers, starting with Eliab, the oldest. Looking at his seven sons, perhaps he reasoned, "Surely God will pick one of these tall, able-bodied, and handsome sons of mine."

One by one these men of stature passed before Samuel, but God didn't pick any of them. Bewildered at God's rejection of all seven brothers, Samuel asked Jesse, "Is that it? Are there no more sons?" Suddenly, Jesse remembered he had one more son, David.

But he wondered why Samuel would even consider David, so he said, "Well, yes, there's the runt. But he's out tending the sheep" (1 Sam. 16:11 MSG). To Jesse, David was the weakest of his sons and not worth their time. To Jesse, David could only look after bleating sheep and was certainly not anyone's choice to rule God's people.

But we know how the day ended. God chose David when he was presented before Samuel, and the prophet promptly anointed the lad as the next king of Israel after Saul. The last became the first.

CHOOSE TO DEPEND ON THE GOODNESS OF GOD AND SEE HIM CHOOSE YOU TO HEAP HIS HUNDREDFOLD BLESSINGS ON.

Like David, you may have been overlooked or rejected by others because of a disability, a stained past, a physical weakness, or a lack of skill. But if you choose to depend on the goodness and kindness of God toward you, you will see God choose **you** to heap His hundredfold blessings on!

GOD TURNS REJECTS INTO CHAMPS

I know what it's like to be sidelined, rejected, and even ridiculed. I was a stutterer and stammerer in high school, and I had one particular teacher who would always pick me—for all the wrong reasons. Whenever he came into the classroom, the first thing he would do was make me stand and read for the sheer pleasure of watching me stutter my way through the passage: "Th . . . th . . . the . . . the . . ." My ears would go red and this teacher would laugh. The boys in the class would laugh with him and the girls would giggle. You can imagine what that did to my self-esteem as a teenager.

Back then, I only knew to call on God for help. I remember how I actually felt sorry for the Lord because now, He had all my weaknesses to deal with. Well, long story short, God took a stutterer and turned him into a preacher with a worldwide platform. The influence and platform I have today, I know it is all God's doing. When I surrendered my weakness to Him, He turned my area of weakness—my mouth—into an area of strength. Never in my wildest dreams did I think back then that I would one day be preaching to millions and seeing lives set free and transformed by the word of grace He puts in my mouth.

And I'm here to tell you that what God did for me, He can and wants to do for you because God is no respecter of persons (Acts 10:34 KJV). In God's economy, the last will be the first. When you bring the Lord into your situation, you won't be facing rejection for the rest of your life. You're having a hard time now because the enemy knows there's something special about you, and he's doing all he can to stop you from becoming the champ God has destined you to be.

God has marked you for great things. He has called you from your mother's womb—you are not a mistake! You have a high calling from heaven and the devil is afraid you'll pick up on it. I believe you were born for a divine purpose and even blessed with special giftings to fulfill your calling. The enemy may have told you you are useless and a hopeless case, but don't give in to these negative thoughts. **God** isn't ever going to give up on you because "God's gifts and his call can never be withdrawn" (Rom. 11:29 NLT). So don't quit now!

YOUR WEAKNESSES QUALIFY YOU FOR GREATNESS

Perhaps you're asking, *"How can God use me when I have so many weaknesses? I have a learning disability. I've been overweight since I was a child. I'm so shy I can't even speak to people without choking in fear. I dropped out of high school and I come from a very poor family."*

Friend, leave all that to God who parted the Red Sea with His breath and who makes a way where there is none. Leave all that to God who raises the dead and makes the lame to walk and the blind to see. Leave all that to the God of the impossible—**your** God—who calls things that are not as though they were. Let me also encourage you with this passage of Scripture that will help you understand whom God chooses:

> I don't see many of "the brightest and the best" among you, not many influential, not many from high-society families. Isn't it obvious that God deliberately chose men and women that the culture overlooks and exploits and abuses, chose these "nobodies" to expose the hollow pretensions of the "somebodies"?
>
> —1 Corinthians 1:26–28 MSG

BY HIS GRACE YOU CAN GO FROM LAST TO FIRST.

Is that you—not among the brightest, the best, or the most influential? Have you been overlooked by others, perhaps exploited and bullied? Do you feel like a nobody every time you're around the somebodies in school, at work, or at family gatherings? Well, you have many reasons to rejoice because according to the portion of God's Word you just read, you are a prime candidate for God's grace. You have exactly the qualities God is looking for to be a mover and shaker in His kingdom. **Your very disqualifications are your qualification**. And by His grace you can go from last to first and be the one He chooses to confound what the world considers wise and mighty!

GIVE HIM YOUR WEAKNESS

How do you begin to walk in favor and experience the breakthroughs you need when your weaknesses are staring you in the face? First, surrender your weaknesses to God. Be honest about your weaknesses. Tell Him, "Lord Jesus, I have all these weaknesses . . . but I'm asking You to use me in any way You see fit. I surrender all my weaknesses, all my faults, all my imperfections to You. I give You my life, and I ask You to do something with it, for Your glory."

Do you know what happens when you are honest about your weaknesses and you humbly give them to Him? His transforming grace and power will rest upon you. The Bible tells us that God gives grace to the humble (1 Pet. 5:5) and His strength is made perfect in weakness (2 Cor. 12:9).

The greatest apostle, Paul, said, "I am glad to boast about my weaknesses, so that the power of Christ can work through me. That's why I take pleasure in my weaknesses, and in the insults, hardships, persecutions, and troubles that I suffer for Christ. For when I am weak, then I am strong" (2 Cor. 12:9–10 NLT). Isn't that amazing? Paul was **happy** to boast about his weaknesses and even **took pleasure** in them!

My friend, when you have a revelation that your weaknesses attract the grace of God and bring His power into your situation, like Paul, you will not feel ashamed or condemned by your weaknesses. When you understand that God's grace is like water that flows to the lowest points, you'll see your weakness as a divine opportunity to allow God's power to flow unhindered through you. He cannot manifest His strength when you are trying to be strong by your own efforts. But when you give it all to Him, He will transform you into a powerhouse for His glory. You can expect God to do great things through you!

GOING FROM LAST TO FIRST

God loves you, my friend, and His way of getting from last to first isn't costly, laborious, or complicated. It is to simply **trust His goodness**. Just believe that God is **really** that good—to you, to your family. Believe He wants to fulfill your hopes and dreams. That's what I want you to see as we take a look at the parable of the vineyard workers. It's from this parable that our Lord Jesus tells us, "So the last will be first, and the first last. For many are called, but few chosen" (Matt. 20:16).

Let me explain right here that Jesus is not saying that only a few would finally be saved and make it to heaven. If you look at the context, He told this parable in response to Peter's question, "We have left all and followed You. Therefore what shall we have?" (Matt. 19:27). Jesus was teaching His disciples what was in store for those who followed Him—the hundredfold return or blessing—and who would be chosen to receive this fullness of His blessings. You see, many are called to enjoy a blessed life in Christ but few **allow themselves** to be chosen for His complete, hundredfold blessings. We're going to see how it is the last and the least that He chooses—when they choose to trust wholly in His goodness.

In this parable, four groups of workers were hired over the course of the day by a vineyard owner. We'll just focus on the first and last groups. The first group was hired early in the morning (before 9am) with the vineyard owner agreeing to pay them each a denarius for a day's work. The last group was hired at the eleventh hour (at 5pm) and worked only for an hour.

At the end of the work day (at 6pm), the vineyard owner began to pay his workers, starting with the **last** group. This group was the last to be hired and worked only one hour, yet they were the **first** to be paid. And not only that, each worker received a **full** denarius—a full day's wage. They got the hundredfold, complete blessing even though they worked for just an hour.

Now when the first group knew about this, they supposed that having worked many more hours, they would get paid much more. But to their surprise and displeasure, the vineyard owner also paid them a denarius each, as had been agreed upon.

HE IS GENEROUS TOWARD YOU

The last became the first—first to be paid and paid a full day's wage. All they did was to trust in the goodness of the vineyard owner. When he hired them and told them, "Whatever is right you will receive" (Matt. 20:7), they didn't get suspicious and cut a deal with him to make sure they would be paid fairly like the first group did. They were just happy to be hired as no one had wanted to hire them. They left it up to the vineyard owner to determine their pay, trusting fully in his goodness and integrity.

And wouldn't you say the vineyard owner was very generous? How many bosses do you know are this generous? When the first group got jealous and angry, the vineyard owner said to them, "Are you going to get stingy because **I am generous**?" (Matt. 20:15 MSG).

The vineyard owner here is actually a picture of our Lord Jesus, and He is a good, generous God. He is kind to the last, the lost, the least. He gives them favor, promotes and blesses them a hundredfold, even when they least deserve it. That's our God! When you choose to rely on your own wits and efforts to secure your blessings, you shortchange yourself from experiencing the fullness of His supply. But when you choose to simply trust His grace and goodness, He chooses **you** to show His generosity to!

IT'S NOT TOO LATE!

Perhaps today you can identify with the eleventh-hour workers. Just as all the other workers had a bigger head start than they, you may feel you're way behind in experience, skills, or qualifications compared to everyone else. Maybe you're a single parent concerned that you have to work extra hard to provide for your children's needs. Or maybe bad choices you've made over the years have taken a toll on your health, finances, and family relationships, and now you are wondering if it's too late to see restoration in these areas.

Maybe you've made many mistakes and feel it's too late now to answer God's call.

WHEN YOU TRUST THE LORD TO BE A GOOD GOD TO YOU, HE CAN PROPEL YOU FROM LAST TO FIRST AND BLESS YOU ABUNDANTLY ABOVE ALL YOU CAN ASK OR IMAGINE.

Friend, God can still "hire" you at the eleventh hour when no one else wants you. He can still step in and bless you even when you think the odds are against you. And He will even give you a full day's wage—a full, hundredfold blessing in your area of need—because He is a good, generous God. Will you believe that for yourself and your situation?

It's not too late. You will not lose out or get left behind indefinitely when you trust the Lord to be a good God to you. He can propel you from last to first and bless you abundantly above all you can ask or imagine because He is **that** good. All He asks is that you trust His goodness. He prizes simple faith in His goodness. When you choose to believe that He is a good God to you, He sees that as faith.

TRUST HIS GOODNESS AND LIVE LESS STRESSED

Are you stressed out and anxious today because you've been trying your hardest to deserve your breakthroughs? Are you exhausted because your best efforts month after month to overcome your weaknesses or lack by your own strength are still not producing results?

Let go and let God, and you'll start to live less stressed. I'm not telling you to live a passive life and not be diligent in cultivating what He's put in your hands. By all means do that, but ultimately, trust His goodness and generosity. Learn to take the humble, lowly position and say, "Whatever is right, Lord, I'll receive from You. I trust Your goodness. I'm depending on Your grace."

When you believe that He is a good God and that He is good toward you, you can leave the details and complexities to Him, knowing that He can give you more than you could ever ask for. I asked God for a wife and He gave me Wendy. Whoa! Friend, He has your best interests at heart and He knows what you need ten, twenty years from now.

When you learn to trust His goodness in all areas of life, day-to-day living becomes less complicated and more relaxed and enjoyable. Despite what you see as weaknesses in your life, you'll find restful increase. You'll move ahead, meet your sales quota, meet your life partner, get that promotion, or see your child do better in school, without all the anxiety and tears. As you trust His goodness and just enjoy the journey, He'll move you from last to first and cause you to run right smack into His hundredfold blessings!

NO MORE ZERO SALES, LESS STRESSED AT WORK

Let me share a testimony with you to encourage you. Jenny, who has been following my teachings in Vietnam, was feeling stressed in her sales job as she had a tough time trying to close deals. After four months, she was still bringing in zero sales, and was conscious that she didn't have what it took to be a top-producing salesperson. "Weekly sales meetings were tremendously stressful for me and I constantly felt hopeless and desperate," she shared.

Initially, Jenny was angry at God because she had prayed and waited, only to be disappointed time and time again. But at her lowest point, she decided to give all her weaknesses to God . . . and began to see God's grace flow in her life. As she learned to talk to the Lord and trust His goodness, He gave her the strength to persevere and the wisdom to change her circumstances. She shared with me, "By the grace of God, I came to terms with my shortcomings as a salesperson. I began to see where to study more about the market and what I needed to improve on."

During this time, Jenny continued to work but with a more restful heart: "I let God work through me, believing He was providing me with His wisdom and blessing the work of my hands. I stopped working with a sense of desperation. I believed the battle was His and it would be pointless for me to even drag a giant sword onto the battlefield with my own hands. I relied on God one hundred percent because victory could only come from Him."

Not long after, Jenny began to see results. She said, "I closed double deals within two weeks and exceeded fifty percent of my target for that month! The greatest lesson I learned was this: only God can give success. We cannot earn or force breakthroughs to happen by our own might. Instead, we can work with a restful, joyful heart and see success because God is faithful. God wants us to trust in Him with all our hearts and lean not on our own understanding."

God kept giving Jenny favor with her clients, moving her up from the bottom position, and causing her to see success in her career. Today, Jenny works with less stress and more results, as she continues to lean on God's grace. She shared, "Now I talk to God every morning before going to work. I would also read daily devotionals to find peace and center myself on God's grace. They help my days go by peacefully and efficiently."

Perhaps you are going through what Jenny did. You've "toiled all night and caught nothing" (Luke 5:5).

GIVE GOD YOUR WEAKNESSES AND WORRIES. LET HIM FIGHT YOUR BATTLE AS YOU SIMPLY REST IN HIS LOVE FOR YOU.

Despite all the hard work you've put into your business, studies, or parenting, you're still not seeing the blessings. Perhaps you're still way behind your competitors, or failing or barely passing your examinations, or not seeing any improvement in your child's behavior. Beloved, like Jenny did, give God your weaknesses and worries. Let Him fight your battle as only He can and simply rest in His love for you. When you begin to trust His goodness and faithfulness, He will give you favor and wisdom. You will surely begin to see results!

JUDGE GOD FAITHFUL AND SEE HIS GOODNESS

Can I share with you one last story to encourage you? You may be familiar with the story of Abraham and Sarah in the Old Testament, and how they could not conceive for decades because Sarah was barren. She was barren when she was young and doubly barren when she was old. Her friends and neighbors probably already had grown-up children while she was still hoping for just one child of her own. It could have been so easy for her to feel sidelined by God.

How did Sarah's miracle come? Hebrews 11:11 tells us: "By faith Sarah herself also received strength to conceive seed, and she bore a child when she was past the age, because she judged Him faithful who had promised." Sarah **judged Him faithful**. That's trusting in the goodness and promises of God. That's how she could supernaturally conceive and give birth to Isaac, through whom not just the Jewish nation, but the promised Seed—our Lord Jesus—would come. She went from last to first because she trusted the goodness of the Lord.

Today, whether you are last in your family, last in class, last in the sales team, or last in traffic, choose to trust His goodness. Believe that He is faithful and good to you. Be like David and say, "I am confident I will see the LORD's goodness while I am here in the land of the living" (Ps. 27:13 NLT). And I believe with all my heart that He will work all things out for your good and propel you from the bottom to the top to have first dibs on His best blessings!

4.

CHANGE HOW YOU SEE, CHANGE YOUR LIFE

He couldn't understand it. Here he was, a man the Lord had called blessed (Gen. 12:2–3), but in the one area that would bring him and his wife greatest joy, they were barren.

This couple, Abraham and Sarah, wanted a child so badly and had spent decades watching other couples having babies seemingly without effort. And still this one blessing kept eluding them. Abraham had even heard the Lord Himself promise: "I will make your descendants as the dust of the earth" (Gen 13:16). Yet up to now, he and his wife couldn't seem to conceive even once.

Maybe right this moment, you understand exactly what Abraham was going through. You know what it feels like to wonder when your breakthrough is ever going to come. Maybe it's been so long, you've given up hope and you don't know how to stay in faith anymore. It could be a lingering health issue that has hindered your enjoyment of life, an addiction you can't seem to quit, or a marriage that's just gotten from bad to worse.

What was God's answer to Abraham?

Long before there were self-help gurus and motivational speakers, God asked a childless Abraham to step out of his tent into the desert night and to look up at a sky filled with stars. Then God gave Abraham a glorious, hope-filled visual of his future: "Count the stars if you are able to number them. So shall your descendants be" (Gen. 15:5).

God's answer to Abraham was to give him a powerful visual for the eyes of his heart. For an eighty-five-year-old man who had been trying for a long time to have just one child with his wife, that must have been such an awesome faith-inspiring picture. But today, that picture is a reality: not only are all Jews Abraham's natural descendants, but all believers in Christ are also his descendants by faith (Rom. 4:16).

My friend, as you're waiting on the Lord for your breakthrough today, would you allow Him to change the way you see your situation, and take you from defeat to victory? What He did for Abraham, He wants to do the same for you!

GOD GOES RIGHT TO THE HEART OF THE MATTER

What image do you have of yourself, your future, or your family on the inside of you? Are they pictures that give you hope? Or are they images of the very things you fear? Do you see yourself healthy, thriving, enjoying life with your family and friends, and serving in church? Or do you see yourself sickly, stuck in a dysfunctional family, always lonely, and full of fear?

Oh Pastor Prince, I don't believe all this visualization stuff. Isn't it a New Age teaching?

No, my friend. Terms like "creative visualization" may have been coined by popular psychology or the New Age movement, but long before the world started teaching about how we can have what we see, God had already put this wisdom into His Word for His children. Why? So He can put His pictures of His abundant life into our hearts and lead us to experience all the blessings He has already prepared for us through Christ's finished work.

We see this principle of seeing His blessings before we possess them right in the book of Genesis when God told Abraham, "I am giving all this land, as far as you can see, to you and your descendants as a permanent possession" (Gen. 13:15 NLT). Whatever of the land Abraham **saw**, and **as far as he saw**, ***that*** he would possess. God in fact told him to "walk through the land in every direction, for I am giving it to you" (Gen. 13:17 NLT).

Why did Abraham have to first walk through the land if God was going to give it to him anyway? Because God wanted him to first see not just with his eyes, but also in his **heart**, every aspect of this land even though it had been promised to him.

And God once again employed this principle when He got Abraham to look at the stars after Abraham became discouraged at having no heir despite God's earlier promise to bless him with descendants as uncountable as the dust of the earth (Gen. 13:16). The stars would come out every night, which meant that every night, Abraham could gaze at them and let what he saw burn a powerful visual in his heart. And from a place of discouragement, this image of the innumerable stars representing his future progeny took him to a place of hope and then faith—an unwavering faith in God's promise that brought glory to God (Rom. 4:18–21 NLT).

My friend, the way God imparts faith to walk out His promises is to give you a picture. And today, He wants you to know He has already put His pictures of your successes, your victories, and your breakthroughs **in His Word**. Your part is to get His visuals deep inside you, right in your **heart**.

THE POWER OF SEEING IN YOUR HEART

The book of Proverbs, where we find His wisdom to walk in His divine health and life, shows how God changes your heart first before He changes the outward circumstances of your life. Look at what Proverbs 4:20–22 says:

> My son, give attention to my words; incline your ear to my sayings. Do not let them depart from your eyes; keep them in the midst of your heart; for they are life to those who find them, and health to all their flesh.

Is there any part of your body hurting or your life not functioning well? God's divine health can touch those areas and heal and restore them. His resurrection life can swallow up every symptom of degeneration and death. But how can this happen? The key is keeping His Word before your eyes and keeping it in the midst of your heart.

You see, when you prioritize "seeing" God's Word, it will drop into your heart. And then, His Word becomes life to you and health to ALL your flesh. This is why God tells us in the very next verse: "Keep your heart with all diligence, for out of it spring the issues of life."

GOD CHANGES YOUR HEART BEFORE HE CHANGES THE OUTWARD CIRCUMSTANCES OF YOUR LIFE.

Beloved, how much life and health you enjoy all spring from your heart. In the same way, sickness, lack, and bondage are many times also birthed first in our hearts. Jesus Himself said, "A good person produces good things from the treasury of a good heart, and an evil person produces evil things from the treasury of an evil heart" (Matt. 12:35 NLT). Many people are unhappy with the kind of health or family life they are seeing right now. What they don't realize is that all these actually proceeded from their hearts.

EVERYTHING PROCEEDS FROM YOUR HEART

In the very first mention of the word "heart" in the Bible, we see how the heart is tied up with our imagination, and that **what we imagine is intricately tied up with how we will live**. Look at what Genesis 6:5 KJV says: "And God saw that the wickedness of man was great in the earth, and that every imagination of the thoughts of his **heart** was only evil continually." As a result of his constantly imagining evil, man's wickedness grew and grew until it was "great."

In the New Testament, our Lord Jesus told the people of His day, "But I say to you that whoever looks at a woman to lust for her has already committed adultery with her in his **heart**" (Matt. 5:28). Notice how Jesus also linked the heart to seeing and imagining. He was telling them that to have those imaginations regarding a woman in one's heart was to already commit adultery with her. In other words, what you imagine in your heart is as good as done.

This is why the devil would love to pollute the imaginations of your heart with pictures of sin, pornography, sickness, and death—because that's how he can produce these evil things in your life. This is exactly why the Lord tells us out of His love and wisdom, "Guard your heart above all else, for it determines the course of your life" (Prov. 4:23 NLT).

He wants to clean up and restore your imagination to operate as He designed it to. And you allow Him to do this when you pray and ask the Holy Spirit to give you His pictures through His Word. When you have His pictures in your heart, you will go on to experience His healing and abundant life.

WANT TO SEE CHANGE? CHANGE WHAT YOU SEE IN YOUR HEART

If you don't like what you see in your circumstances today, what can you do about it?

My friend, change what you see on the inside with God's pictures. Replace those old, negative pictures in your heart with new faith-filled ones from His Word, and your situations and life will begin to change for the better.

Are you feeling exhausted from the demands of work and family? Maybe you are recovering from a serious illness that has left you feeling weak. I encourage you to get your Bible and meditate on this uplifting picture painted for you in Isaiah 40:31 NIV: "Those who hope in the LORD will renew their strength. They will soar on wings like eagles; they will run and not grow weary, they will walk and not be faint."

As you meditate on these words, see them applying to you. See the Lord lovingly imparting His divine strength and vigor to your body. See yourself so strong and so full of His life that you are soaring over fatigue, over discouragement, and over the symptoms in your body. Pretty soon, strength will come into your body and mind, and you'll find yourself walking without fainting, and running without feeling weary!

IF YOU DON'T LIKE WHAT YOU SEE IN YOUR CIRCUMSTANCES TODAY, CHANGE WHAT YOU SEE ON THE INSIDE.

Perhaps you've been feeling discouraged and defeated lately over bad decisions you've made. Instead of seeing yourself forever trapped in lack, sickness, or bondage as a result of your mistakes, see how much He loves you, has forgiven you, and how much of a victor you are over your situation through Christ who loves you.

This is what Edith from Texas did. When she first began watching my program on television, she was, in her own words, "completely strung out on drugs." She shared:

It was a normal thing to get high with the family members and people I hung out with. Although I had a deep desire to break away from it, I was never able to.

I remember how I felt when I heard Joseph Prince speak continuously about how much God really loves me and how He is not disappointed with me despite my mistakes.

I began visualizing in my spirit and believed with my heart that I was freed from my addiction. *I found the courage to go to church and that helped me overcome my fears and doubts. Finally, I also stopped hanging out with negative people in my life and was completely set free from drugs.*

Nine months later, I met the man of my dreams. I'm now married by the grace of God and I've remained clean for five years now. Pastor Prince's preaching of God's love has set me free!

Praise the Lord! Edith's breakthrough came when she understood how much God loves her and began seeing herself free of her addiction. This faith-filled picture gave her hope as well as the courage to surround herself with the right community, to stop hanging out with those who had a negative influence in her life, and to experience lasting victory and much more. My friend, the same kind of breakthrough and victory can happen for you!

GOD'S HEART FOR YOUNG PEOPLE

What kinds of pictures and images are you filling your heart with? Are they filling you with hope and purpose, or are they filling you with insecurity, anxiety, and fear? Beloved, it is so important for you to guard what you allow into your heart because the pictures you see in your heart will determine the course of your life.

If you're a young person and reading this, listen. The enemy is all out to capture your heart, so guard what goes through your eye-gate in this day and age. He knows that if he can corrupt your imagination through what you see, he can lead you down the path of addiction, defeat, and depression. So be careful what you let into your heart via the internet and social media. Don't allow him to pervert your values and beliefs, and ultimately, the course of your life through false success pictures, pornography, and other negative images.

We live in a society that is so dependent on social media and our smartphones that we've developed FOMO disease. FOMO is the Fear of Missing Out. We must check every update. Every "ding!"—every notification—must be checked, and it must be checked *now*! That's living a very stressful and very sad life.

THE BEST WAY TO COUNTER NEGATIVE IMAGES OF YOURSELF AND YOUR LIFE IS TO HAVE FAITH-FILLED PICTURES FROM GOD'S WORD.

People put up the best pictures of themselves, and if they don't get enough likes, they feel so crushed that they take down their pictures. It's very much a false world because most people only post the highlights of their lives. Everyone is comparing and competing, and the need to be liked has resulted in people, especially the young, having low self-esteem and negative images of themselves and of life.

The best way to counter all the negative images is to have faith-filled pictures from God's Word. Our heavenly Father wants the imaginations of our hearts to be flooded with light from His Word. The apostle Paul put it this way: "I pray that the eyes of your heart may be enlightened, so that you will know what is the hope of His calling" (Eph. 1:18 NASB).

FAITH PICTURES FOR A STUTTERER

Let me share with you my own story of the faith pictures God had put in my heart when I was a youth. I've shared that I used to stammer and stutter. Even when I was in high school, it was a challenge for me to stand in front of a crowd and speak. I was ashamed and I was afraid.

I remember the first time I had to stand and speak before a crowd. I asked the Lord, "Help me! Give me a verse." And the Lord gave me Jeremiah chapter 1.

Now the prophet Jeremiah was a young man, probably a teenager when God first called him. And God knew he was feeling extremely inadequate for the job and afraid of the people he had to speak to. So God said to him, "Say not 'I am a youth,' . . . prepare yourself and arise, and speak to them all that I command you. Do not be dismayed before their faces" (Jer. 1:7, 17).

God was telling me the same thing, and He gave me three faith pictures in the next verse: "For behold, I have made you this day a fortified city and an iron pillar, and bronze walls against the whole land" (Jer. 1:18).

Wow! The Lord saw me as a "fortified city," "an iron pillar," and a "bronze wall"!

Now I had no problem envisioning a fortified city, so I began to see myself strong, stable, and secure—someone others could turn to in times of crisis. But I had to learn to see myself as an "iron pillar" and a "bronze wall"—a person of strength, not easily taken down by negative things people said about me.

As I kept meditating on these faith pictures, my fears started to melt away. Whenever I had to stand up and speak before a group of people, I would no longer be afraid of what I saw on their faces. These faith pictures have truly transformed me and enabled me to preach to thousands on a weekly basis.

What the Lord did for me, He can do for you too. Whether it's a fear of public speaking, a health issue, or an addiction, God wants to change you from the inside out. And He starts by dropping faith pictures into your heart. That's why He gave you the Bible. It's His picture book to transform your heart.

THE BIBLE IS GOD'S PICTURE BOOK TO TRANSFORM YOUR HEART.

So let Him change what you see. Find a faith picture from the Bible that speaks to you about your situation, meditate on it until it becomes a vivid picture in your heart, and see it happening to you or for you. As the negative pictures in your heart get replaced with faith pictures from God's Word, you will start to see positive changes in your life!

FAITH PICTURES FOR YOUR HEALTH FROM THE WORD

Perhaps you've just heard a bad medical report from your doctor and the enemy has got you playing the worst-case scenarios in your heart, over and over again. Perhaps you are afraid of growing old and getting sick and can't help but see depressing inward pictures of yourself aging, falling sick, and wasting away.

Beloved, the Lord loves you and wants you to live a long and fruitful life. Instead of negative images, He wants you to have this faith picture in your heart:

> He shall be like a tree planted by the rivers of water, that brings forth its fruit in its season, whose leaf also shall not wither; and whatever he does shall prosper.
>
> —Psalm 1:3

That's how the Lord sees you. That's how I see you too, not in the natural, but through the eyes of God. More importantly, **you** have to see yourself as an evergreen tree planted by rivers of water that brings forth fruit in its season. You are **planted** by Him who loves you. You are not there by accident. And He has planted you by **rivers** (plural) of water. You are surrounded by rivers of living water that supply all your needs. You will not dry up or wither, and you will be fruitful. Whatever you do shall prosper. "Whatever" means that even if you make a mistake, our Lord Jesus will work it out for good!

And as you anchor your heart on the powerful Word of God, align also your words with what you see in this faith picture. Get into the habit of declaring Psalm 1:3 over yourself and saying, "Like Moses at one hundred and twenty, my eyes will not be dim nor will my natural vigor be diminished" (Deut. 34:7). You will see God's promise for you come to pass: "As your days, **so shall your strength be**" (Deut. 33:25)!

FAITH PICTURES FOR FAMILY LIFE

Did you know that God's Word is also full of faith pictures for a blessed family life? If you've been struggling in your relationship with your spouse or children and have come to see them negatively in your heart, let the Word of God give you new pictures of your loved ones.

Husbands, start to see your wife as the virtuous woman of Proverbs 31.

But Pastor Prince, you don't know my wife! She's not like that!

God says, "I see her as one," just as how He saw Gideon as a "mighty man of valor" even when he was afraid and hiding from the enemies of Israel (Judg. 6:11–12).

God always calls things that are not as though they were, like how He changed Abram's name to Abraham (Gen. 17:5), calling him "father of many" when the man was still childless! And because Abraham believed God and received that picture into his heart, his situation changed.

Do the same with your wife. See her as the Proverbs 31 woman and as a fruitful vine (Ps. 128:3). See her as someone who intoxicates you. You are not too old and it's not too late to start!

What about your children?

God's Word says that your children shall be "like olive plants all around your table" (Ps. 128:3). Why olive plants? Because God wants you to see your children as **anointed**. They have the oil of God on them. Olive oil from the olive plant is one of the ingredients of the holy anointing oil (Ex. 30:22–25). So their peers out there may be stressed and cynical but your children are anointed with God's peace and hope.

My friend, our children are different. Always see them as different. Believe the best of them, even when it comes to their teenage years. Believe they are anointed to make the right decisions.

See your children having eyes anointed to see the goodness of the Lord, ears anointed to hear the words of Jesus and His love. Their hearts are anointed to discern truth from lies. Even if your heart is troubled right now by the poor decisions they have made, believe they are anointed to reach their God-given destinies.

And having God's anointing always makes everything easy.

Let me ask you this: Your door hinges creak, why? No oil. Your joints creak, why? No oil. There is friction in your relationships, why? No oil. When there is oil, when there is the Lord's anointing, there is no friction and strife. So believe the Lord anoints your spouse and children, see them through His eyes, and see Him bless your family relationships.

GUARD YOUR HEART AND SEE RIGHT

What are you seeing on the inside today? Do you see your loved ones saved even though they may seem opposed to the things of God now? How do you see your country? How do you see yourself?

Many of us have cultivated a logical mind for so long, we need the Holy Spirit to revive His gift of imagination in us and resurrect the dreams He once put in our hearts. That is what I'm praying for you today. I'm believing that He will flood with light the eyes of your heart to see every challenge working out for your good, and to see your health, your family, and your future through eyes of faith.

Do you remember God saying to Abraham, "All the land which you **see** I give to you" (Gen. 13:15)? Because we are Abraham's descendants through faith in Christ, hear the Lord saying to you also, "All you SEE, I give to you."

My friend, are you ready to start changing your circumstances? Then start changing what you see in your heart and let God's faith pictures change your life!

5.

SPECIALLY PROTECTED TO LIVE UNAFRAID

Luke was twenty-four years old, healthy, and had recently celebrated great news with his family—God had opened huge doors of opportunities and favor for him, and he had been promoted to a coveted position in his company. The last thing he was expecting just one day before he was to start work in this new position was for a cab to ram straight into him while he was using a crosswalk in the middle of the city.

Luke was thrown onto the hood of the cab, before landing on the street. Dazed but not knocked out by the impact, Luke slowly sat up, checked himself . . . and realized that miraculously, he had not sustained any injury—not a single broken bone, bruise, or scratch! Baffling onlookers who had gathered around him in concern, he got on his feet and walked away.

When his family members heard about his accident, they urged him to go to the hospital for a thorough checkup. But Luke refused, insisting he was completely fine. Two weeks later, he continued to be injury-free, assuring his mother on one occasion, "Mom, I am one hundred percent fine. I just went to the gym and got a monster lift in!"

Unknown to Luke, on the morning of the accident, his mother,

Brenda, had felt led to pray God's protection from car accidents over her children. It was, in her words, "not something I usually do." But somehow, the Lord had led her to hear my message on Psalm 91 and His protection. Later that afternoon, when Brenda received a text message from Luke telling her about the accident and that he was totally fine, she fell on her knees and cried tears of joy. She thanked her wonderful Father God for His protection over her son and for the leading of the Holy Spirit to cover him in prayer.

"I used to pray Psalm 91 over my family all the time, but over the years, I had forgotten about this powerful psalm," Brenda said in her email to me. "Thank you for reminding me of the power of Psalm 91. When we pray the Word of God over our children or any situation, we release His angels to work on our behalf. Praise the Lord!"

What a powerful testimony of the Lord's protection! Not only is it a timely reminder of our need for His protection in every area of life, it also reveals God's heart to protect and deliver us. As a parent, I rejoice with Brenda over the Lord's protection of her son and believe that the Lord will cause Luke to be a testimony of His goodness and grace in his workplace and everywhere he goes!

WE NEED GOD'S PROTECTION

I shared Luke's testimony with you to show you that we all need God's protection. Luke was just crossing the street, minding his own business, yet found himself right in the path of trouble. He never thought that he would be the innocent victim of a car accident while doing something as mundane as crossing a street.

ONLY GOD CAN SEE INTO THE FUTURE, ORCHESTRATE EVENTS, AND DIRECT OUR STEPS SO THAT WE END UP IN THE RIGHT PLACE AT THE RIGHT TIME.

Nobody wants to be at the wrong place at the wrong time or in harm's way. Sure, we can plan ahead and take precautions, but all our "wise" planning cannot guarantee that we will always be at the right place at the right time. Only God can ensure that. Only God can see every snare the enemy has set for us (Ps. 91:3). Only God can see into the future, orchestrate events, and direct our steps with impeccable precision so that we end up in precisely the right place at precisely the right time—all the time—and He is more than willing and able to cover us and our loved ones with His 24/7, all-round protection!

SAVED BY THE TRUE PILLAR

You may have heard me share in my messages about how one of our church members survived the 2003 Marriott Hotel bombing in Jakarta, Indonesia. Just before noon on August 5, a suicide bomber detonated a car bomb right outside the lobby of the popular Marriott Hotel, killing twelve people and injuring 150. This church member was in Jakarta for a business trip, stayed at the Marriott, and was in the hotel's lobby when the bomb went off.

The explosion tore through the lobby, shattered glass, and threw people off their feet. This brother even saw a body flying past him as the deafening blast reverberated all around him. After the dust had settled, he found blood splattered on him and debris strewn all around, but amazingly, he was completely unhurt. At the very moment when the bomb exploded, he "happened" to walk behind a pillar that protected him from the impact of the blast. The pillar, or I should say, the true Pillar (Ex. 13:21), saved him. Talk about God directing your steps and putting you at the right place at the right time!

I remember reading reports describing how the bombing was planned in secrecy and with meticulous detail days ahead to achieve maximum impact. But because "the eyes of the LORD are in every place, keeping watch on the evil and the good" (Prov. 15:3), He was well able to guide and protect this church member. My friend, only God, who sees all, can give us the complete protection we need. Only He can place us at the right place at the right time, protect us, and cause us to walk away totally unharmed!

YOUR HEAVENLY FATHER WANTS TO PROTECT YOU

It doesn't take much to see that we are living in troubling times. You only have to watch the news channels for a couple of minutes to see that the world is plagued by dangers and destruction—wars, earthquakes, hurricanes, deadly viruses, terrorist attacks, senseless killings, travel disasters, road accidents . . . the list goes on. In the recent global battle against the COVID-19 pandemic, we saw how not just lives, but jobs were also lost at an alarming rate. The bottom line is, we need God's all-round protection now more than ever. But the good news is that as believers in Christ Jesus, we have a heavenly Father who loves us and is more than able to protect us and our loved ones.

Parents, we can't always watch over our children's every move and ensure that they are safe everywhere they go. Only God, being omniscient and omnipotent, as well as all-loving toward us, can give us and our loved ones all-round protection, round the clock. If we love our children and don't want any harm to come upon them, how much more our heavenly Father, who loves them more than we ever can? Our part is simply to believe in His sure promises for us found in His Word and rest in His steadfast love for us.

Is there such a promise of protection for us in the Word to anchor our hearts on today? Yes, there is! Look with me at Psalm 91, the Father's awesome psalm of protection for us:

> He who dwells in the secret place of the Most High
> Shall abide under the shadow of the Almighty.
> I will say of the LORD, "He is my refuge and my fortress;
> My God, in Him I will trust."
>
> Surely He shall deliver you from the snare of the fowler
> And from the perilous pestilence.
> He shall cover you with His feathers,
> And under His wings you shall take refuge;
> His truth shall be your shield and buckler.
> You shall not be afraid of the terror by night,
> Nor of the arrow that flies by day,
> Nor of the pestilence that walks in darkness,
> Nor of the destruction that lays waste at noonday.
>
> A thousand may fall at your side,

And ten thousand at your right hand;
But it shall not come near you.
Only with your eyes shall you look,
And see the reward of the wicked.

Because you have made the LORD, who is my refuge,
Even the Most High, your dwelling place,
No evil shall befall you,
Nor shall any plague come near your dwelling;
For He shall give His angels charge over you,
To keep you in all your ways.
In their hands they shall bear you up,
Lest you dash your foot against a stone.
You shall tread upon the lion and the cobra,
The young lion and the serpent you shall trample underfoot.

"Because he has set his love upon Me, therefore I will deliver him;
I will set him on high, because he has known My name.
He shall call upon Me, and I will answer him;
I will be with him in trouble;
I will deliver him and honor him.
With long life I will satisfy him,
And show him My salvation."

Beloved, this is God's Word for His precious children. He wants you to anchor your heart on His powerful promises in this psalm. I encourage you to take some time right now to just speak this psalm over yourself, your loved ones, or your situation. Whatever your fears, let the many reassuring promises of protection found in this one psalm alone bring strength, peace, and comfort to your heart and mind.

PROTECTED 24/7 FROM EVERY HARM AND EVIL

Every single promise in Psalm 91 is ours, when we, like the psalmist acknowledge our need for the Lord and His protection. You will see His intervention and deliverance when you "say of the Lord, 'He is my refuge and my fortress; my God, in Him I will trust.'" Instead of saying, "*Well, you never know, que sera, sera, whatever will be, will be*" or "*It's up to me to take care of myself and my family,*" He wants us to say, "Lord Jesus, I can't protect myself or my family the way You can. So I take You as our refuge and fortress. My trust is in You and not my intelligence, skills, experience, or careful planning."

LEARN TO SAY, "LORD JESUS, I CAN'T PROTECT MYSELF OR MY FAMILY THE WAY YOU CAN. SO I TAKE YOU AS OUR REFUGE AND FORTRESS. MY TRUST IS IN YOU."

As our loving Father, God is pleased when we allow Him to take us under His protective wings, the way a mother hen spreads out her wings to protect her chicks from danger. Psalm 91 shows us that God wants to and will protect His children from whatever harm the enemy can come up with. Are you afraid of unseen deadly viruses and diseases that threaten to take up residence in your body? Well, His Word in Psalm 91 promises that He will "deliver you from . . . the perilous pestilence . . . You shall not be afraid . . . of the pestilence that walks in darkness," and that "no evil shall befall you, nor shall any plague come near your dwelling."

Maybe you've been hearing news of how a deadly virus has been claiming lives and spreading far and wide, and fear has begun to creep into your heart. Perhaps doctors have told you that a certain disease runs in your family and you're afraid that you'll contract it. Beloved, let the Word of the Lord guard your heart. He who does not give empty guarantees says to you, "A thousand may fall at your side, and ten thousand at your right hand; but it shall not come near you." Instead of playing the worst-case scenarios in your head, see yourself covered by and taking refuge under His wings. Whatever may have happened to others, God promises in His Word that He will deliver and protect you, satisfy you with long life, and show you His salvation.

What if you live in an area where the crime rate is high and violence of some form, such as drive-by shootings, is common? Take heart, my friend, for His Word also says that you "shall not be afraid of the terror by night, nor of the arrow that flies by day." And what He did for our church member who was shielded from the flying shrapnel of the bomb blast, He can do for you too—"He shall deliver you from the snare of the fowler . . . He shall cover you with His feathers, and under His wings you shall take refuge; His truth shall be your shield . . . You shall not be afraid of . . . the destruction that lays waste at noonday." Hallelujah!

Whatever the threat, fear, or danger, your Daddy God has you covered from every angle! I encourage you to study and meditate on Psalm 91, especially if you tend to worry over the safety of yourself or your loved ones. Speak this psalm over your life. Pray this psalm over your family every day and sense your Father's love for you and your loved ones.

If you and your family need to travel and you are concerned about health and safety, just speak this psalm over yourselves. And if you're afraid of flying, take a moment to remember His promise of protection and sense His love for you. Before you board the plane, say, "Father, I'm Your child and I know You love me. Thank You for keeping me in the secret place of the Most High. When I board this plane, You board the plane with me. Thank You for keeping me safe." See your heavenly Father spreading out His mighty wings of love and protection, and trust Him to take good care of you and yours every moment of the trip. That's how you can relax and enjoy it, free of anxieties and fears.

PROTECTED THROUGH THE STORM

Let me share with you a testimony that bears out what I just said. Regina, a mother of two from Virginia, had planned to take a road trip with her daughters within the United States. A few days before the trip, this mother felt a prompting to read Psalm 91 with her children. They read the psalm of protection together, speaking aloud the many promises of God. Regina also read the psalm every night to her girls as they drifted off to sleep. Yet, in all of that time, it never crossed her mind that she would be very close to "one of the biggest tornado outbreaks in the history of the United States."

Some hours into the very first day of their road trip, as they drove through Virginia and Tennessee in their SUV, this family encountered horrendous weather conditions—heavy dark clouds, with strong winds and hail. Yet, every moment that she had to drive through the storm, Regina felt the Lord's protection on her family and their vehicle, and His peace guarding her heart.

Emerging unscathed from the storm, Regina and her girls stopped to eat in north Georgia. Regina wanted to hurry through their meals so they could get back on the road as soon as possible before the weather worsened. But she felt the Lord telling her to slow down and to let her girls take their time and enjoy the food. When they finally finished their meals and left the restaurant, Regina felt further impressed to fill up at the gas station next door. She honestly didn't see the need to, but to be obedient to the prompting within, she did it anyway. Then, they got back on the highway and continued their trip.

After travelling less than a mile, the traffic came to a complete stop. Very quickly, Regina realized that something serious had just happened right up ahead. Only minutes before, a large tornado had torn through the town directly ahead of them! It had caused massive destruction on the very section of the highway that they were mere minutes away from. Regina said, "By God's grace, the Lord had us stop to get food and gas, slowing us down enough to keep us from encountering the destructive tornado! We missed the tornado by only three to five minutes! True to His Word, the Lord kept us safe throughout our entire trip!" Regina shared happily. I praise the Lord for His protection over this precious family. Only He could have known that a tornado was coming up ahead, and guided this family so that they were always protected and at the right place at the right time, out of harm's way.

SET APART FOR SPECIAL TREATMENT

My friend, as a believer in Christ, you don't have to live in fear like the people of the world. You can expect to live differently—above dangers and storms of any kind, because you have God's Word that

He will protect and deliver you and keep you, His beloved child, safe. As His children, we may be in the world, but we are not of the world (John 17:11, 14). We are set apart from the people of the world unto Him. We are "His own special people" called "out of darkness into His marvelous light," through faith in the shed blood of His Son (1 Pet. 2:9)!

AS A BELIEVER IN CHRIST, YOU CAN EXPECT TO LIVE ABOVE DANGERS AND STORMS OF ANY KIND, BECAUSE YOU HAVE GOD'S WORD THAT HE WILL PROTECT AND DELIVER YOU AND KEEP YOU SAFE.

You see this truth in action during the time of great famine in the book of Genesis when Joseph, after being promoted by Pharaoh, prepared a special place called Goshen for his family. What was so special about living in Goshen? We see the answer in what Joseph told his brothers: "You shall dwell in the land of Goshen, and **you shall be near to me, you and your children, your children's children . . . There I will provide for you**" (Gen. 45:10–11).

Today, through the finished work of our Lord Jesus, our heavenly Joseph, God has placed us in *Goshen*, which means "drawing near."[1] This is the place we have in Christ, where through His blood, we've been brought near to God. It is a place where we enjoy an intimate relationship with Him, and where He provides for us and protects us as He has promised in Psalm 91.

Now, look with me to see how God made a difference between His people in Goshen and the Egyptians when terrible plagues came upon Egypt because Pharaoh stubbornly refused to release God's people from slavery. Through Moses and Aaron, God told Pharaoh, "And in that day **I will set apart the land of Goshen, in which My people dwell**, that no swarms of flies shall be there, in order that you may know that I am the LORD in the midst of the land. **I will make a difference between My people and your people**" (Ex. 8:22–23).

We see from the account of the ten plagues how, not only were God's people free of the swarming flies, but when all the livestock of the Egyptians died, none of the livestock of those living in Goshen did. And when there was hail in all of Egypt, there was no hail in the land of Goshen. Similarly, when thick darkness swallowed up the land of Egypt, "all the children of Israel had light in their dwellings" in Goshen (Ex. 10:23).

Beloved, our God, who is the same yesterday, today, and forever, makes a difference when it comes to His people! This is the reason you and I, as His beloved children in Christ, need not live life fearful, afraid to travel, or always worrying about our children and our needs. Even if economic uncertainties or increasing terrorist activities beset the world, because we know we are near to Him and dear to His heart, we can face life with boldness. We can live each day free from stress, well protected and well taken care of, because we have a Daddy God who sets us apart as "His own special people." You and I are special to Him and we have His personal attention and protection!

PRAYER FOR GOD'S PROTECTION

When you know how much your Father in heaven loves you, you don't have to depend on your own limited intelligence or resources for your blessings and protection. You can rest in His unfaltering and unfailing love and protection for you and your family.

Would you at this moment allow me to pray with you? Today, if there are concerns and fears weighing on your heart, know that God is your comfort, your strength, and your protection. All you need to do is acknowledge your need for His protection and take Him as your refuge and fortress. As we pray the words below together, see Him covering you under His mighty wings:

> Father God, thank You for loving me and giving up Your Son, Jesus, to die for my sins so I can be blessed with every blessing, including 24/7 protection. I acknowledge that my family and I need You and Your all-round protection in our lives and in every challenge that we face. I thank You that day or night, whatever and wherever the snare, YOU are our refuge, our fortress, our shield, and our deliverer. I thank You for Psalm 91 that not only promises protection and deliverance for Your people, but also a long and satisfying life. My family and I can face life with boldness and enjoy peace, because You are our heavenly Father who loves us intensely, watches over us carefully, and directs our steps perfectly. Thank You for placing all of us under the shadow of Your wings and for always putting us at the right place at the right time. In Jesus' name, amen!

My friend, your Father in heaven loves you and wants to set you apart as a testimony of His faithfulness and goodness. Go forth today with the assurance that you and yours are favored and protected to freely live to the fullest the abundant life that His Son died to give you!

6.

THE POWER OF REST IN A CRISIS

She never expected this would ever happen—her only son dying in her lap after taking ill suddenly while playing in the field.

Without a word, she laid her child to rest on a bed in an upper room and closed the door behind her. Then she asked for a donkey and servant so she could quickly go to the prophet, Elisha. She hoped and believed that this man of God would bring her son back to life. When her husband asked her what was going on, she didn't tell him what had happened and instead said, "It is well."

If there was one woman who kept her cool in the midst of a crisis, it was this Shunammite (2 Kings 4:8–37). Make no mistake, her soul was "in deep distress." But on the surface, she just kept uttering three words: "It is well." In today's slang, "It's cool." In Hebrew, the single word *shalom*, meaning "peace."[1]

Most folks in her situation would have been hysterical. But this woman kept her composure throughout. With the minutes ticking by as her son lay cold and motionless at home, she stayed focused with those three words from her spirit and on the single objective of meeting Elisha, God's answer then for her crisis.

This Old Testament story has a happy ending as you may already know. When the life went out of her son, this woman chose to put her trust in the Lord and rest in His grace and His power to restore her son back to her. The result? She experienced a most extraordinary miracle against all conceivable odds!

RESPOND WITH REST IN A CRISIS

My friend, what I want you to see today is this: what you decide to do in a crisis matters.

When mitigation measures and restrictions were announced in response to the coronavirus outbreak, one of the first things that happened was chaos in supermarkets worldwide. From America to Australia, checkout lanes packed with hundreds of shoppers and rows of empty shelves that had held milk, bottled water, and toilet paper reflected the uncertainty and fear people felt as the virus escalated into a global health crisis. Triggered by negative news, dread of worst-case scenarios, or just seeing other people rushing to buy essential items, normally sane people joined the fray of panic buying that ended up creating a vicious cycle of shortages and more fear.

When we are faced with a crisis or any situation that spells danger or an uncertain and frightening future for us, I know it's hard not to feel anxious. And when fear and anxiety hits, instinctively, we all feel we need to do something quickly to avert a negative outcome. It's hard not to try to find out all we can in order to **do** all we can in an attempt to feel safe and secure.

But the Lord has a higher way for us. He doesn't want us to **react**; He wants us to **rest**.

GOD DOESN'T WANT US TO REACT IN A CRISIS; HE WANTS US TO REST.

You might understand the word "crisis" to mean a situation of instability, danger, and distress, a situation fraught with difficult circumstances. But did you know that *crisis* also means "the **turning point**" in a stressful situation?[2] Beloved, I believe that when you learn about and take up the Lord's invitation to rest in Him in the midst of your crisis, you will see a turning point, a change in your circumstances. You will see the Lord turning every negative thing around for your good.

Maybe you're going through a season of uncertainty and anxiety today. Maybe you've just lost your job, or all signs point to you possibly losing your job. Maybe you've just had a bad report from the doctor, or your marriage is crumbling around you and there doesn't seem to be any way to save it.

Whether it's a health crisis, financial crisis, relationship crisis, or all three rolled into one mega storm, I want you to know the Lord who faced the ultimate crisis of the cross loves you and cares deeply about you. He wants you to know He's right there with you as you're trying to navigate your way in this storm and He's waiting for you to invite Him into your boat. Invite Him in as His disciples did one dark, stormy night and watch Him calm the sea and winds and bring you to your desired destination (Mark 6:51, John 6:16–21).

My friend, the Lord isn't distant and indifferent. Even if it feels like He's "asleep" in your boat and you're about to go under, just one cry from you, and He will arise. He will rebuke the storm—"Peace, be still!"—and usher into your situation a great calm (Mark 4:39). You don't need to feed endlessly on the news or internet articles and social media, looking in vain for that "miracle cure" to your problems. You don't need to go around in circles trying to make headway in your situation all by yourself. When you choose to rest in His love and in His finished work that has secured your protection and provision for every need, that's when you'll receive your miracle and come out stronger, higher, and better in every way.

POSITION BEFORE PROVISION

Imagine being in the wilderness with 5,000 men, not counting the women and children. It's late afternoon, the sun is setting, and the bellies of the folks are growling. And as you know, hungry folks aren't the happiest folks. But how are you going to feed all of them, if all you have for food is one kid's modest lunch?

You are probably familiar with the miracle of the feeding of the five thousand that's recorded for us in all four gospels. Our Lord Jesus miraculously multiplied the five loaves and two fish of a boy's lunch to feed the entire multitude. But have you ever noticed what **posture** the people were in when they received all the food they could possibly eat?

Before multiplying the food, Jesus said to His disciples, "Make them sit down." Did you get that? They were all to be **seated**! To be seated is to be in a position of rest. My friend, this is the truth I want you to see: **position before provision, rest before receiving**.

Perhaps you are facing a crisis of lack today. You can't fulfil the orders flooding in and customers are starting to post negative reviews and comments. Or maybe there's just not enough in your bank account to pay for last month's school fees even, not to mention your other outstanding bills. Maybe there's a dangerous virus going around and you're worried your body doesn't have sufficient immunity against it.

My friend, I know it goes against logic and every inclination in your body, but the Lord wants you to sit down and rest. Rest and receive what you need from your Savior. I'm not talking about literally sitting down and doing absolutely nothing. Rest is not inactivity but Spirit-led activity. Rest means bringing the Lord into your crisis as you do what you need to. It means casting every care to Him. It means asking Him to lead you one step at a time to your breakthrough and doing what you sense His Spirit prompting you to do.

REST MEANS BRINGING THE LORD INTO YOUR CRISIS AS YOU DO WHAT YOU NEED TO.

My friend, even if you have to call 911 or drive a loved one to the ER, you can do it with rest. Take a breather and pray. "Be still, and know that I am God" (Ps. 46:10) means He wants you to take a moment to remember He is the God who will fight for you, rescue you, and deliver you. Let Him restore your peace and sanity and impart the wisdom you need. Even as you do the necessary, be restful inwardly like the Shunammite woman, knowing the Lord has got this and is with you and for you every step of the way.

In the book of Isaiah, the Lord reminds us, "Only in returning to me and resting in me will you be saved. In quietness and confidence is your strength" (Isa. 30:15 NLT). Having the strength to overcome your adversity and being delivered from your crisis have to do with turning to the Lord and resting in His love for you. His peace comes into your heart and mind and quiets the turmoil within when you turn it all over to Him and rest. How? By making all your needs known to Him (Phil. 4:6).

Jesus cares affectionately about you, and He wants to take all your burdens and replace whatever lack you have with His abundance (1 Pet. 5:7, Phil. 4:19). Be at rest, my friend, and as in the miracle of the feeding of the five thousand, receive His miraculous, more-than-enough provision.

JOB RETAINED, BONUS RECEIVED

Let me share a testimony that I pray will encourage you today, especially if you're worried about your job.

Bernice, a lady from Missouri who follows my ministry, was sure she would lose the job she loved. Extremely troubled by this, she would wake up at night, attacked by fear. But watch how the Lord kept Bernice's job intact and even caused her to receive a hundredfold blessing:

> *Shortly after the Lord blessed me with an amazing career, my boss informed me that he was planning on leaving because of stock ownership issues. The business would be dissolved and my boss advised me to contact my recruiter and jump ship before it sank. That night, I cried the whole way as I drove home.*
>
> *Feeling defeated, I began applying for jobs and going for*

interviews. Throughout this painful process, I was partaking of the holy Communion and agreeing with Jesus for His best in the situation. At night, I would sleep holding on to Jeremiah 29:11 as I kept waking up attacked by fear.

At some point, I discovered that the stock ownership conflict had originated because someone greedy was stirring up problems. Once I learned that, I was only going to release my miracle job if it was God Himself moving me. I declared in Jesus' name that the enemy would not destroy the company. I also asked the Lord to release the annual employee bonuses that had not been distributed due to all the chaos.

About a month later, everything turned around miraculously. The negotiations changed so completely in my boss' favor that he took over the business. And he awarded me a bonus, the exact amount of the sign-on bonus I received when I started with the company. It was an unequivocal miracle on top of a miracle.

What a turnaround! Bernice rested by holding on to God's promise as she partook of the Communion. The result? The business conflict was favorably resolved, and Bernice got to keep her dream job. On top of that, she was awarded a sizeable bonus. Friend, even though it all looks like a big, bad mess, the Lord can turn the whole situation around so that when the dust settles, you are left standing poised—with even more supply in your possession!

DIVINE PROTECTION BEGINS WITH REST

If you're going through a personal crisis and trusting the Lord to protect you and your loved ones from a bad outcome, I want you to see that as with provision, **protection** also follows the position of rest. Let's look at Psalm 91. I love studying this psalm for its powerful secrets and promises on the Lord's protection. Not long ago, He showed me how His all-encompassing protection also begins with the humble posture of being **seated**.

Right from the start, the psalm says, "He who dwells in the secret place of the Most High shall abide under the shadow of the Almighty" (Ps. 91:1). "He who dwells" comes from the single Hebrew word *yashav*, which means "to sit down."[3] The very first word in this go-to psalm for God's protection invites us to **sit down**!

The Lord's emphasis here is rest instead of restlessness. Deliverance from the snare of the fowler, the perilous pestilence, the terror by night, the arrow that flies by day, the destruction that lays waste at noonday, the lion and the cobra . . . all begin with rest!

There are believers who think their protection lies in simply confessing Psalm 91, as if it were a magic formula. When something bad happens to them, they think, *"Oh, it's because I didn't confess Psalm 91."* When they're afraid of something bad happening, they confess Psalm 91 mechanically, believing it is their act of confessing that keeps them safe. But that's not what **sitting down** or **dwelling in the secret place** means.

So how do you "sit down" when you are assaulted by fears for yourself or your loved ones? This is what I do: I bring my family before God in prayer and I tell Him, "Father, thank You that in Christ, I am seated in the secret place of the Most High. I thank You that my family and I are seated with Christ, far above every principality and power. We are under the shadow of the Almighty. We are safe under Your wings."

IT'S HIS FAITHFULNESS (NOT YOUR OWN) THAT KEEPS YOU FROM EVIL.

You see, Psalm 91 isn't something magical. It's not something you trot out, confess a few times, and expect protection to just happen. No, it's having a revelation of the safe and secure position you are already in through our Lord Jesus' sacrifice at the cross and resting in **His** faithfulness (not your own) that keeps you from evil. Jesus gave up His position of divine protection when He took your sins and mine at the cross. He became cursed so that you and I could always walk under God's 24/7, all-round covering today. And the more you meditate on this revelation and walk it out, the more restful you'll be, and the more you'll see His protection manifest tangibly in your circumstances.

PROTECTED FROM COVID-19

At the start of the COVID-19 outbreak in Singapore, the Lord had me teach what I just shared with you about Psalm 91. Let me share with you a testimony from Amy, a lady from my church, who continued to run with this message of rest even when she received alarming news from the health authorities during this epidemic.

Unknowingly, Amy attended a business meeting where she came in contact with a person who later tested positive for COVID-19. She shared candidly how fear crept into her heart when, during her stay-home period, she found out that a colleague who attended the same meeting had succumbed to the virus and was seriously unwell: "I started to get paranoid as I kept hearing about new cases in Singapore each day."

I want you to see what Amy did in response to the fear and how her story ended:

> *I listened to Pastor Prince's sermons and also read his book* Eat Your Way to Life and Health *again. I prayed that my colleague who had tested positive would be the last person from the business meeting to be infected. I also claimed the promises of Psalm 91 over me and my family.*
>
> *Eighteen days later, my family and I remained healthy. None of us came down with the virus. God is truly our protector!*

Praise the Lord! Friend, the enemy's strategy is always to move you out of peace and rest into fear and stress by flooding your mind with worrisome thoughts and worst-case scenarios. I'm so glad that when he tried to do that with Amy, she chose to stay in rest—she talked to the Lord, listened to the Word, and reminded herself of what Jesus' finished work had accomplished for her. Armed with renewed faith, she declared the Lord's powerful promises in Psalm 91 over her situation.

I'm sure it must have been unpleasant for Amy, who had been trusting the Lord from Day 1 of the epidemic, to hear that she had come in contact with a person who tested positive for COVID-19. Notice that Amy didn't spend time asking, *Why did this happen to me?* and become even more anxious. Instead, when she caught herself being fearful, she chose to fix her eyes on the Lord and rest in His faithfulness to keep her and her family safe no matter what had happened. And when she rested in Him, she and her family tangibly experienced all His promises in Psalm 91.

Likewise, you may have been trusting the Lord for a situation and perhaps it hasn't improved or seems to have gotten worse. Beloved, whatever may have happened, continue to remain in rest.

Like Amy, refresh your heart with a fresh revelation of the Lord's love for you by hearing of the gospel and partaking of the Lord's Supper. And like Amy, you'll see the Lord protecting you, straightening the crooked paths, and leading you out of your trouble.

FEEDING IS FIGHTING

Beloved, no matter how bleak your crisis may look today, your only fight is to remain at rest. Even though you have not seen your breakthrough, even though the healing has not manifested, tell the Lord, "Lord Jesus, I thank You. I'm at rest because You are fighting this battle."

Let me show you a powerful truth to resting and seeing the Lord fight your battle for you. It's found in the Hebrew word for "fight." Did you know this word—*lacham*—means "to do battle" as well as "to eat"?[4] *Lacham* is also where we get *lechem*, or "bread."[5]

Now why would God put the ideas of **feeding** and **fighting** within the same word? Because He wants us to know this: we don't fight by fighting. We fight by **feeding**. That is how we remain at rest. That is how we allow the Lord to work unhindered in our crises. And that is how we experience victory in our battles.

We feed on our Lord Jesus, our bread of life, and the enemy is defeated. I've lost count of the number of times our church members have told me how they came to church to feed on the Lord and His love through the preached Word . . . and went home to find their troubles resolved. They discovered that as they fed, He fought for them and took care of their problems.

WHEN YOU FEED ON JESUS, THE BREAD OF LIFE, HE FIGHTS FOR YOU AND TAKES CARE OF YOUR PROBLEMS.

When you feed on Jesus, the bread of life, and on His gracious words and powerful promises, you are not doing nothing. You are **already** fighting the enemy and all that he is doing. But it's not the kind of fight where you rely on your own strength and feel weary and stressed out with no victory in sight. There's a rest because the battle truly is the Lord's, and you are drawing on His power, His wisdom, His anointing, and His unmerited favor as you simply feed on His words that will not return void!

BANK ON YOUR SHEPHERD'S FAITHFULNESS

Whatever crisis or adversity you may be facing today, I'm believing with you that you **will walk through** the valley of the shadow of death (Ps. 23:4). You are not camping in your crisis. That is our Lord Jesus' promise to you today because He is your Good Shepherd. He is with you even as you go through the valley, using His rod and staff to defend and protect you. You don't need to live anxious or afraid. You don't need to fight. As we see in the opening verses of Psalm 23, the beautiful Shepherd's psalm, all He wants for you, His sheep, is just to **lie down** in green pastures.

Green pastures speak of an abundance of what a sheep needs to thrive. I believe that as you take up His invitation to **lie down**—as you rest in His love and faithfulness—you'll find Him leading you, protecting you, and supplying you with everything you need. He will restore your soul, deliver you, and cause His goodness and mercy to surround you. My friend, as you remember to rest by feeding at His table in the presence of your enemies, you will be refreshed and strengthened. Fresh hope and faith will be imparted to you. And you will emerge victorious because the battle is the Lord's!

7.
EXPECT TO RECEIVE GOD'S MUCH-MORE RESTORATION

She was young, married for a few years, and looking forward to a blissful family life with children of her own. Then, the unthinkable happened—her husband suddenly died. Overnight, all her hopes came to naught; her future, uncertain. Although her mother-in-law urged her to return to her own town to start afresh, the young woman refused. Clinging to her mother-in-law, she said, "Wherever you go, I will go. Wherever you lodge, I will lodge. Your people shall be my people, and your God, my God."

With these words, one of the most beautiful love stories in the Bible—the story of Ruth—unfolds. Beyond being just a love story (that is also a picture of our redemption in Christ), it is also a heartwarming story of God's amazing restoration.

When Ruth followed Naomi, her mother-in-law to Israel, she soon found herself in a less-than-ideal position. She was a Moabitess among a people often in conflict with Moab, and had no husband to protect her. In the natural, it seemed as if the odds were stacked against her as she started life in her new community.

But Ruth didn't dwell on her unfavorable circumstances. Her declaration of her faith in the God of Israel before she even left Moab revealed her dependence on the Lord, whom she looked to for favor and divine opportunities. "Please let me go to the field, and glean heads of grain after him in whose sight I may find favor," she said to Naomi one day (Ruth 2:2). Her trust in the Lord as she embarked on the ordinary task of finding work to support her mother-in-law and herself became her launching pad to God's incredible restoration in her life.

First, God gave Ruth favor to glean the barley harvest in the field of Boaz, a wealthy man who **happened** to be a close relative of her late husband. Boaz was extremely kind to Ruth, allowing her to gather more than enough grain in his field for both her and her mother-in-law's daily needs. But God had more in mind than mere survival for Ruth. He blessed her with a husband—Boaz himself—and with a child, Obed, who became the grandfather of King David and whose name was recorded in the ancestry of Jesus Christ. Ruth herself is named in the genealogy of our Lord Jesus.

When it seemed impossible in the natural, Ruth's life went from empty to full. Imagine going from having no family to having a loving husband and son, from being destitute to being well-provided for. And from being an outcast to being not just an accepted and well-loved member of society, but also part of the lineage of the Messiah Himself. What a turnaround! What amazing restoration!

RESTORATION OF LOST YEARS

Maybe you can identify with what Ruth had gone through before she met Boaz. Maybe you're at a place where your hopes have been crushed. Perhaps a series of events have shattered your dreams and left you with a bleak future. Maybe you're saying to yourself, *"It's over for me!"*

My friend, I have good news for you today: **God wants you to know that it's not over**. Don't give up; your situation is not hopeless. His powerful restoration is on the way! Take heart as you hear His Word to you:

> I will restore to you the years that the swarming locust has eaten, the crawling locust, the consuming locust, and the chewing locust.
>
> —Joel 2:25

Beloved, because our Lord Jesus has purchased every blessing, including restoration, for you at the cross, you can believe God to redeem all the time that has been wasted and lost. God's heart is to restore to you whatever the locust—a picture of the enemy—has eaten, **especially** your lost years. If you've been living in regret over years lost to addiction, depression, or a never-ending series of failures, God is willing and able to turn things around for you.

OUR GOD IS A GOD OF RESTORATION AND HE IS MOST ABLE AND WILLING TO RESTORE WHATEVER YOU HAVE LOST!

No man can do this but the Lord. He lives outside time and can supernaturally restore to you all the wasted time you have spent in fear, worry, doubt, guilt, condemnation, sickness, and bondage. Whether you have lost precious time, a relationship dear to you, or if you've suffered a debilitating illness that has robbed you of your health or your youth, let His Word strengthen your heart today. Our God is a God of restoration and He is most able and willing to restore whatever you have lost!

Let me encourage you with a testimony that I received from Stephie to show you that God, who changed the life of Ruth, is still restoring precious lives today.

Stephie was just eight years old when her parents were divorced. It broke her heart and started her on a journey of deep insecurity. She left school at the age of thirteen, began taking drugs and watched her life spiral out of control after that. By the time she was sixteen, she was in prison after having tried every new drug available and selling them at the nightspots she worked at. In and out of prison over the next few years, she always returned upon her release to the drugs that held her captive. Then one day, Stephie's addiction got to crisis point—she developed a severe infection resulting in a drastic loss of weight, loss of hair, and a loss of strength and ability to work on a business she'd started. In sharing what life was like for her during that time and how her turnaround happened, she said:

> *I often felt angry with myself for what was happening, and I would flush the drugs down the toilet bowl. However, I would give in within half a day. I knew I needed help but didn't know where to get it.*
>
> *Then, a friend brought me to New Creation Church and that changed my life forever. After attending church for a few weeks, I woke up one morning with clarity of mind. I finally realized that the "cursed" life that I thought I had was already taken away from me. I had found grace.*
>
> *With this fresh revelation, I prayed to God to help me overcome my addiction. Whenever I felt the urge, I just declared, "I am the righteousness of God in Christ." I stopped relying on my own willpower and just told God, "I cannot, but You can."*

My drug addiction grew worse initially and my family and boyfriend lost all patience with me. The small business I had at that time was also not doing well. Everything in my life was so wrong. Still, I continued praying and telling God, "I really don't know what to do, but I am relying on You."

One fine day, the drug that I was addicted to ran out of stock. I was desperate and worried about the effects of withdrawal on my body. My sister, who also attends New Creation Church, prayed for me and partook of the holy Communion with me.

Amazingly, after two weeks, I still did not have any withdrawal symptoms, and I realized I was totally set free from drug addiction! The infection I was suffering from was also healed during one of the extended worship sessions led by Pastor Prince. And when the drugs I was addicted to came back into supply a month later, by God's grace I no longer had any desire to go back to them!

Today, I am happily married with two kids and blessed with a thriving business. I am healthy, my hair has grown, and I feel and look so much better. I am so blessed to also be serving in church.

I am so grateful and humbled by the fact that God did not spare His own Son for my sake. I can't imagine where I would be without my Savior, the Lord Jesus Christ.

What a precious testimony of how our Lord Jesus can restore all that the locusts have eaten! If you, like Stephie, have experienced years lost to addiction, sin, or sickness, don't remain in discouragement or become bitter or believe that there is no more hope for you. Like Stephie, choose to tell Jesus, "Lord, I cannot, but You can. You can restore to me time that's been lost. You can restore to me everything the locusts have eaten."

And God will surely bring about His much-more restoration of years lost, His renewal of your mind and body, and even a deeper relationship with Him. He who loves you and gave His only Son to die for you will make things right, and give you **more** than what was lost or stolen. Whatever the enemy meant for your harm, God can take those experiences and turn them around for your good!

RECEIVE HIS MUCH-MORE RESTORATION

Let me show you from the Scriptures that when God restores something, His restoration is always greater in quality or quantity or both. Whatever the enemy has stolen from you, you can believe God for a 120-percent restoration.

Why 120 percent, Pastor Prince?

Because it is based on the principle of restitution in the law of the trespass offering found in Leviticus 6:4–5: "Then it shall be, because he has sinned and is guilty, that he shall restore what he has stolen, or the thing which he has extorted, or what was delivered to him for safekeeping, or the lost thing which he found, or all that about which he has sworn falsely. He shall restore its full value, add one-fifth more to it, and give it to whomever it belongs, on the day of his trespass offering."

Here, we see God's law detailing what a person must do to provide restitution to someone he has injured. Notice this law states that he "**shall restore its full value, add one-fifth more to it, and give it to whomever it belongs.**" The full value of whatever was lost, defrauded, or stolen plus one-fifth is 120 percent of the original value. Now, this principle of restoration was under the old covenant of the law. How much more we who are under the new covenant of grace—a far better covenant with God, based on better promises (Heb. 8:6)—can trust God not just for a 120-percent restoration but much more!

Notice also that the person brings his restitution on the day of his trespass offering. The trespass offering is a picture of what Jesus did for us at the cross. He became our substitute and was judged in our place for every trespass we committed so that we can freely receive every blessing of God, including the blessing of His much-more restoration. Today, even if your losses are a result of bad decisions you made, you don't have live consumed with regret and hopelessness. The Lord is saying to you, "Let go of the past. I paid for those mistakes as your substitute, and I will restore to you what you have lost and more!"

IF THE ENEMY HAS STOLEN THE BEST YEARS OF YOUR LIFE, GOD IS GOING TO RESTORE TO YOU AND MAKE YOU A GAINER. YOUR BEST DAYS ARE AHEAD OF YOU!

Friend, if you have accepted Christ as your trespass offering, I pray fresh hope is entering your heart now to believe that His 120 percent restoration is coming your way. If the enemy has stolen from you or defrauded you of the best years of your life, then in that very area that you have suffered loss, God is going to restore to you more than you had before. He is going to restore to you the years the locusts have eaten, and according to His principle of restitution, make you a gainer. Your best days are ahead of you!

EXPECT TO BE A GAINER

In the same way the Lord didn't want Ruth to just survive, He doesn't want you to just live through a miserable marriage. He wants to turn it around and restore to you a loving, intimate relationship with your spouse. Similarly, He doesn't just want your business to stay afloat, He wants your business to thrive! He doesn't just want you healed, He wants you healthier than before! Our Lord Jesus never brings us out the same. He will **increase, improve, promote**, and make everything better.

Even if you've made some poor decisions, don't feel condemned. Instead of indulging in self-pity or regret, turn to your Savior and say, "Lord, restore!" and expect things to change in your favor. When you put your trust in Him, nothing in your life is beyond restoration. Despite how impossible the situation looks, God is for you and will never give up on you!

If you feel you have been have robbed—of good health, of experiencing wholeness in your relationships, of opportunities in your workplace or career, know and believe that your loving Savior's heart for you is to restore to you much more than you have lost. Believe that He can and will make you a gainer because of that loss. Let me show you another scripture to establish your heart in this truth.

Look with me at Exodus 22:1—"If a man steals an ox or a sheep, and slaughters it or sells it, he shall restore five oxen for an ox and four sheep for a sheep." What do you notice—where the loss is greater (an ox compared with a sheep), the restoration is also greater! God is in effect saying, **the greater your loss, the greater His restoration** to you will be! It may come through the agency of man, but it is the Lord who plans, orchestrates, and brings His much-more restoration to pass in your life. And can you imagine the joy of the man who received five oxen when he had originally lost only one? He was probably happy to have lost that ox because he became a gainer after such a restoration.

YOU DON'T HAVE TO ACCEPT DEFEAT OR LIVE IN DESPAIR. JUST REST IN HIM AND HUMBLY LOOK TO HIM FOR YOUR SUPPLY AND RESTORATION.

So, don't be afraid if there is an area of your life that is under attack. You don't have to accept defeat. You don't have to live in despair. God wants you to rest in Him and humbly look to Him for your supply and restoration.

POSITION YOURSELF FOR RESTORATION

Beloved, the restoration that Ruth and Stephie received can happen for you too. Whatever you have lost, don't give up—you can still win even after you've experienced loss. How? Position yourself for victory by resting in the Lord's finished work, remembering that Jesus has accomplished everything for you at the cross. If you look at the word "restore," it starts with four letters that spell "**rest**." In other words, restoration comes as you rest in the Lord and in His finished work. When you rest in God, He goes to work on your behalf and you end up with more. This was what happened for Ruth, whose story you read about earlier.

After laboring in the barley fields from morning to evening, Ruth was able to glean one ephah of barley (Ruth 2:17), equivalent to a ten-day supply. But when she rested at the feet of Boaz and did not labor, she received six ephahs of barley (Ruth 3:15), a sixty-day supply! And we know her blessings did not stop there. She received a marriage proposal from Boaz—a stable, honorable, affluent, and the most eligible man in the community. How did that happen? Ruth had heeded the advice of Naomi, her mother-in law, to "**sit still**" and wait, after Boaz had promised to redeem her. I want you to pay attention to what Naomi said to Ruth: "Sit still, my daughter, until you know how the matter will turn out; for the man will not rest until he has concluded the matter this day" (Ruth 3:18).

As long as Ruth rested, Boaz would not rest until he resolved her situation. The result? Instead of just getting a small portion of the barley from the fields, Ruth got the owner of the fields himself, as well as the entire yield of his barley fields! Hallelujah! It is the same for us today. When we rest, Jesus, our heavenly Boaz, goes to work. When we choose to "work" by striving, fretting, and trying to make things happen by our arm of flesh, He rests until we see our need for Him and invite Him into our situation.

REST AND RECEIVE HIS RESTORATION

Now, in case you're wondering, rest is not doing nothing or being lazy in your situation. Do the practical that needs to be done—send out your résumés, attend interviews by all means—but do all that with a heart that is at rest. Be at rest inwardly, believing in your heart that our Lord Jesus has accomplished everything you need for every demand that comes your way. Rest in His faithfulness to fulfill His promises to you and to be your supply, strength, and peace while you are waiting on Him. Your restoration can happen when you least expect it, just like it did for Lorraine who wrote to me from North Carolina:

When I was thirty-five, I began losing my sight due to an eye disease called retinitis pigmentosa. By 2006, I could only see with my left eye, with my scope of vision limited to the diameter of a drinking straw.

Round about that time, I began watching Joseph Prince on television. Through the messages that he preached, I learned about Jesus and Abba, my loving heavenly Father. I began to learn all that Jesus endured at the cross for me and how much He wanted a relationship with me. I began watching the broadcast daily and I would search my Bible in Braille over and over in utter disbelief. Could it be true, that by His stripes, I have been healed—even my eyes? I began to claim this verse for myself. I figured I couldn't lose anything since I was already blind.

My husband, Jack, would sit and watch Joseph's programs with me in the mornings. One day, after having listened to Joseph for five months, I told Jack while watching the screen, "Stop scratching your head!" Jack turned to me and said, "How could you have seen that?" That's when I realized that my vision had been restored. I raised my hands to the sides of my face and I could see them!

I went to my neuro-ophthalmologist, who specializes in the disease I was diagnosed with, and asked him to re-run all the tests. Needless to say, he was blown away. I now have near perfect vision—20/20 in my left eye and 20/30 in my right! I soon found out that my type-two diabetes and hypertension have also been healed!

My friend, Lorraine's amazing breakthrough began when she simply sat down to learn about Jesus and His finished work. By doing that, she positioned herself to receive His restoration for her! The Lord restored not just her vision, but also other areas of health that had been compromised by serious illnesses. I believe Loraine is enjoying a fresh flood of His healing and health because she learned to rest and rejoice in God's grace for her rather than focus on what the enemy had stolen from her. So don't be discouraged by the challenges you see in your circumstances. Don't be alarmed even if you should hear bad news. Each time your heart is troubled, look to your unfailing Savior and say, **"Lord, restore!"**

YOUR RESTORATION CAN HAPPEN WHEN YOU LEAST EXPECT IT.

Beloved, I want to encourage you to get ready for an incredible time of God's restoration! Instead of saying it can't be done, start saying, "Lord, restore!" because His sacrifice at the cross has qualified you to receive and enjoy His incomparable restoration. Through the cross, He has restored to you and your family 120 percent and more of His health, soundness, protection, favor, wisdom, and provision. Like Ruth who went from empty to full, I believe you will say in the days to come, "The Lord has turned my loss around with His restoration!"

8.

THE KING WHO CAME TO SERVE

He is the Good Shepherd who leaves the ninety-nine sheep to look for that one lost sheep.

He is the God of all creation, God Almighty, yet He knows you intimately by name and even bothers to number the hairs on your head.

While others are ready to condemn and ostracize the guilty, He is ready to forgive and save them, and in doing so He transforms their lives.

My friend, I am talking about our Lord and Savior, Jesus Christ. He debunks all typical religious notions. To know Him is to say with the psalmist, "Who is there like You, O Lord!" (Ps. 89:8).

Our Lord Jesus is the King of heaven and yet in His own words, He "did not come to be served, but to serve, and to give His life a ransom for many" (Mark 10:45).

Beloved, are you in need of a breakthrough? Perhaps healing of a chronic, painful condition? Or creative ideas for your failing business? Maybe it's restoration of a family relationship that's going from bad to worse.

Whatever your burden, I want you to know that the Lord Jesus came to love you and to serve you. I pray that as you read on, you will come to see this amazing Bible truth and have your walk with Him refreshed. This simple but profound truth will invigorate your heart with hope and reignite your faith to receive from Him the blessing you need!

"WHAT DO YOU WANT ME TO DO FOR YOU?"

Many people think that the Lord Jesus demands this and that of them, that He requires them to sacrifice much for Him and to serve Him tirelessly. Yet, as we have seen from Mark 10:45, He came to serve us, not to be served by us.

In fact, right after our Lord declared this truth, we see a clear demonstration of it. In the same chapter, Jesus came to Jericho and as He was leaving the city, thronged by a great multitude, a blind beggar named Bartimaeus was sitting by the road. When he realized that Jesus was passing by, he began to cry out, "Jesus, Son of David, have mercy on me!"

Many in the crowd told him to be quiet, but he cried out even more. Now, blind Bartimaeus must have known something about Jesus to be so bold in calling out to our Lord despite the crowd's displeasure. I reckon he knew that Jesus could and **would** serve him in the area of his need—recovery of sight.

And the words of this blind beggar caused God Himself, the one who flung the stars, the sun, and the moon into place, to **stand still**! The Bible says Jesus "stood still," called for Bartimaeus to be brought to

Him, and asked him, "What do you want Me to do for you?"

Can you imagine that? The most powerful being in the universe heard the cry of a blind beggar, stopped in His tracks, and responded to the man by essentially asking him, "How can I serve you? What can I do for you?" To which, Bartimaeus replied, "That I may receive my sight."

The Lord's answer? "Go your way; your faith has made you well," Jesus told him in response to his request. And the Bible tells us that "immediately," Bartimaeus received his sight and followed our Lord on the road.

My friend, like Bartimaeus, do you know with certainty that you can reach out boldly to the Lord today? It may look like the forces against you are completely out of your control and that there is no hope for you. Don't lose heart, my friend. Our Lord Jesus wants you to call on Him and hear Him say to you, "What do you want Me to do for you? How can I serve you?"

CALL OUT TO THE LORD TODAY. HE LOVES YOU AND IS MORE THAN WILLING TO HELP YOU.

Go ahead and ask of Him. Ask Him for freedom from that addiction, that long-term health condition, or that mental oppression. You can also ask the Lord for wisdom in your career or studies. Maybe what you need is peace, patience, and strength to love and raise your kids well, or restoration in an area of loss, whether it's an estranged family relationship or lost years due to a string of bad decisions.

Call out to the Lord today. He hears you and He will stand still for you. He wants you to know He loves you and is more than willing to help you!

WHY YOU CAN CALL ON HIM

But Pastor Prince, you don't know what I've done. You don't know my past. I don't deserve God's help.

Neither did blind Bartimaeus. And you are right. I don't know what you've done or what happened in your past. But I can assure you that Jesus does. And His Word assures us that when He went to the cross, He dealt perfectly with the payment and punishment of all the wrong that you and I have done and will ever do (Col. 2:13). I submit to you that when the Bible says your sins are forgiven because of Jesus' sacrifice, from God's perspective, your sins **are** forgiven!

You don't have to do something for God to love you. He already demonstrated His love for you when He gave up Jesus for you. And He knows you by name. He knows the number of hairs on your head. His love for you is that personal and intimate.

You may ask, *How can God Almighty, who has billions of people on the planet to love, still love me with such personal knowledge?* That's why He is God! And He wants you to pray knowing that as you call out to Him, all His love is converged on you. It goes completely against the religious ideas people have of God and prayer, but that's the attitude that delights Him when you talk to Him.

WHAT ABOUT SERVING GOD?

Wait a minute. All this sounds like you are encouraging us to go to God only to receive blessings. What about us serving Him?

My friend, did you see how once Bartimaeus received his sight, he used it first of all to follow Jesus? No one had to preach to him about pursuing the Lord. The moment he had been loved, served, and blessed by the Lord, he willingly and without hesitation followed the Savior!

And that's how our service to the Lord ought to be—out of the overflow of receiving His love for us. Jesus Himself said, "Freely you have received, freely give" (Matt. 10:8). We can only give freely of ourselves to God, to His work, and to people He loves (not grudgingly or out of obligation or a misplaced fear of His judgment) when we first freely receive His love.

Over the years, I have received many testimonies from believers who had sincerely wanted to serve the Lord in church and ministry but became exhausted physically and burned out spiritually because they began with the wrong premise. They believed that they had to serve God before He would love and bless them. And so they did it out of obligation, out of their own strength, self-efforts, and self-sacrifices.

That was the case for Penny, who wrote in from North Carolina. She shared that she had received the Lord when she was ten and how she tried to be good, to study the Bible, to be more involved in ministry, and to "live up to the church's demands of following Christ." There was a lot of service but little or no joy. Then in her thirties, her marriage failed, leaving her devastated, and she became involved in meaningless relationships. She said, "I cried out to the Lord to help me although I had little hope that I would ever be truly whole or happy."

That was until Penny came across my ministry and learned about and understood the differences between the old and the new covenants, and all that Jesus had done for her on the cross. The more she saw the Lord's mercy, grace, and love, the more she fell in love with Him and became passionate about sharing His love with others. With much joy she said:

> *Today I am a writer and Bible teacher who shares with anyone who will read or listen to the message of freedom we have through the finished work of Christ. I am happy and completely in love with Jesus, my bridegroom. He has brought me to a blessed place described in Isaiah 61:3—He has given me a crown of beauty instead of ashes, the oil of joy instead of mourning, and a garment of praise instead of a spirit of despair.*

All glory to our Lord Jesus! Now perhaps like what Penny shared earlier, you have been doing your best to serve the Lord in various capacities, only to feel drained, unhappy, and confused as to why you are even feeling this way. Maybe like her you have been hurt by others and are experiencing one bad break after another.

Beloved, can I ask you to cease from your works and self-efforts to please the Lord and make things right and to just rest and trust in His grace? I believe He is reaching out to you now, washing your feet and refreshing your weary soul with His love. And as you allow

Him to serve you and pour His grace upon you, I have no doubt you will be reinvigorated and strengthened. You'll find clarity and wisdom imparted to you, and in good time you will serve Him again, this time with boundless energy and joy and for all the right reasons!

GET FILLED FIRST

I hope you are beginning to see that even though we want to serve the Lord and we consider it a great honor and privilege to do so, in reality, it all begins with letting Him serve us. And He serves us first with salvation, until we are so full that we are able to serve out of that fullness. This is exactly what happened with the Samaritan woman at the well in John 4.

Her story captures so beautifully our Lord's heart to love and serve us. Remember that our Lord was sitting at the well because He was tired. Even then, He was ready to serve. Our Lord ministered so tenderly to this woman, who because of her immoral lifestyle came to get water from the well at noon—after all the other women had left. She didn't know that she was actually being served by the Messiah, but boy, was she served!

Not only did our Lord Jesus remove her shame and condemnation but He also restored her confidence and self-worth. Now what happened to this woman who, up to that point, had lived a life shrouded in shame? The Bible tells us that after she encountered the Lord and was so full from His ministry of grace, she became an evangelist immediately. In fact, she was so effective that "many of the Samaritans of that city believed in Him because of the word of the woman who testified." You can read all about it in John 4:4–42.

THE SERVANT HEART OF OUR LORD JESUS

To show you how much our Lord Jesus loves you and wants to tend to your needs, let me show you a beautiful picture of Jesus that the Father has hidden in the Old Testament. It is in the law of the Hebrew servant, which is found in Exodus 21, just after God gave the Israelites the Ten Commandments:

> Now these are the judgments which you shall set before them: If you buy a Hebrew servant, he shall serve six years; and in the seventh he shall go out free and pay nothing.
>
> —Exodus 21:1–2

In Israel, every seventh year is a Jubilee year, where every debt is cancelled and everyone is restored to his or her family. Those who had forfeited their lands because of poverty or debts would get their lands back. So Jubilee is a time of freedom and restoration.

The law goes on to say that if the Hebrew servant entered his master's service by himself, he would leave by himself, and if he came in married, then his wife would leave with him. However, "if his master has given him a wife, and she has borne him sons or daughters, the wife and her children shall be her master's, and he shall go out by himself" (Ex. 21:3–4).

That meant that the Hebrew servant had to leave his wife and children behind. But the law also allowed him to choose to stay with his master and family, a decision that required his ear to be pierced:

> But if the servant plainly says, "I love my master, my wife, and my children; I will not go out free," then his master shall bring him to the judges. He shall also bring him to the door, or to the doorpost, and his master shall pierce his ear with an awl; and he shall serve him forever.
>
> —Exodus 21:5–6

Now the door or doorpost is where the Hebrew servant will come so close to freedom—liberty on the outside; servitude on the inside. If he chooses to stay because he loves his master, as well as his wife and children, then his master will bring him to the judges and the doorpost, and pierce his ear with an awl, and he will serve his master for the rest of his life.

Imagine how elated and secure the Hebrew servant's wife and children would feel when they see his pierced ear and the bloodstains. They would know that he could have left to enjoy a life of freedom without them but he chose a future with them. From then on, whenever they looked at his ear, they would see the mark of his piercing and they would remember that he had a choice, and that he chose to stay with them, to be with them, and to take care of them because he loves them.

Isn't that just such a beautiful picture?

It's a picture of our Lord Jesus, who had His hands and feet pierced for us. He is the Hebrew Servant, who left heaven and came down to earth with the sole purpose of fulfilling His Father's salvation plan for us.

The Lord of glory, the God of heaven and earth, came down as a man to serve us by saving and delivering us from sin and from ourselves.

Oh, such humility, that the eternal God would confine Himself in a baby, in time and in space!

At any point during His earthly ministry, Jesus could have chosen to return to His Father in heaven. He could have drawn the line when the religious leaders rejected Him. He could have put His foot down when they plotted to kill Him. Even in the garden of Gethsemane, when the soldiers came to arrest Him, our Lord could have summoned twelve legions of angels and gone back safely to His Father.

So our Lord had a choice—He could return to heaven or He could stay the course and go to Calvary to suffer a most painful death. Our Lord chose to stay. In the language of the account of the Hebrew servant, He said, "I will stay. I love My Master, My Father in heaven; I love My wife, the church; and I love the children, the believers as well as the children of Israel." And He steadfastly set His face to go to Jerusalem where He would die for us and fulfill His Father's will.

Now, because Jesus chose the scourging and the piercings, we can be healed, made whole, and receive eternal life. Because He shed His blood, we can be made righteous, forgiven of every sin. Because He became poor on the cross, we can be well-supplied for every need. And because He wore the crown of thorns, we can be free from mental oppression, anxiety, and defeatist thoughts. Hallelujah!

WILL YOU LET HIM SERVE YOU TODAY?

My friend, Jesus came to serve you. He wants you to receive from Him.

Will you do that today? Will you let Him serve you and turn your situation around for your good and for His glory?

Jackson, a young man living in Australia did just that and found his life wonderfully transformed. At 17, he was "insecure, severely depressed, and suicidal." He partied, experimented with drugs, and tried psychology to feel better. He also tried to be a "good" Christian to get God to hear his prayers and help him.

Nothing worked until Jackson received a revelation of the servant heart of the Lord. Here's what Jackson wrote:

> *I was in the darkest period of my life and had barely a glimmer of hope. But little did I know that at this time, God had already begun His plan to rescue me. He began to unveil Jesus through Pastor Joseph Prince's sermons and resources.*
>
> *I have received the greatest revelation of God's grace and have been tremendously impacted by Jesus' unconditional love and unmerited favor. I now know that I am the righteousness of God through Jesus Christ, the one and only who could ever possibly make it so. I also know that I can always run to Him anytime, anywhere, in any situation, and He will receive me with open arms because* ***He carries a burning desire to help, care for, and bless me****.*
>
> *Today, I am currently planted in a local church, happily and fruitfully serving in various forms. All high-fives to Jesus!*

Praise the Lord for another precious life transformed! My prayer is that you will walk away with the same revelation that Jackson has of the servant heart of Jesus—"He carries a burning desire to help, care for, and bless me."

SEE HIM NOT JUST AS GOD ALMIGHTY BUT ALSO AS YOUR SERVANT-KING WHO WANTS TO PROVIDE FOR YOU AND DELIVER YOU FROM EVERY TROUBLE.

Every day, whether it's through reading your Bible or listening to a sermon or worship song, fill yourself up with the Lord's love and be satisfied by His grace. See Him not just as God Almighty but also as your Servant-King who wants to provide for all your needs and deliver you from every trouble. That way you will run on the power of His love instead of your own human strength, which will only lead to stress and fatigue. That way you will see His wisdom flow in every situation you face and His provision more than meet any need you have!

CLOSING WORDS

Dear friend, I pray you've been blessed by the messages in this book. I pray that in reading about our Lord Jesus' wonderful provision through the cross to supply your every lack, strong Bible hope has been steadily entering and filling your heart—for your health, your family, your future, and every situation you are trusting God for.

I pray you have come to see that whatever your struggle is and no matter how long it has been, it is not bigger than the Lord's love for you, nor His desire and ability to give you a breakthrough and a brand-new start.

Would you give me this opportunity to pray a blessing over you right now? I believe the Lord is with you, wherever you are, to impart the God-kind of hope in your heart for your future and for every prayer that is yet unanswered.

> Father, I thank You that You have prepared days full of blessings for every single person reading these words right now. Because of Jesus' finished work for them, they are standing right now on grace ground, favor ground. And because of this, they can have a positive expectation of the glory of God being fulfilled in their bodies, their marriages, their parenting, their careers, their finances, and their ministries. They can boast in this hope that Your goodness and glory will manifest tangibly in their lives.
>
> Father, for everyone who is hurting and suffering in any area, for everyone battling discouragement, depression, and disease, may they

know that You are in control, that You are with them even now, and that You will lead them safely out of the valley. That supply is coming for every lack and restoration to every broken and painful relationship.

Right now, Father, may You strengthen them to know that in their current suffering, You are imparting to them strength, character, and faith to believe there will be no danger in their future. Only Your shalom-peace, protection, and well-being. When they go to sleep at night, they will not be plagued by worries and anxiety, but their sleep shall be sweet, and they will wake up to see new blessings and fresh protection and provision.

Thank You, Father, for the harvest of good things and breakthroughs You have prepared for them in the days to come. In Jesus' name, amen!

My friend, even as you receive this prayer into your heart, may our Lord Jesus inundate you with His hope today and in the days ahead. And may you find His divine hope becoming an anchor for your soul (Heb. 6:19), causing you to always see His grace, mercy, and help in time of need!

NOTES

Chapter 1: Hope That Doesn't Disappoint

1. OT: 85, James Strong, *Biblesoft's New Exhaustive Strong's Numbers and Concordance of the Bible with Expanded Greek-Hebrew Dictionary*. Copyright © 1994, 2003, 2006 Biblesoft, Inc. and International Bible Translators, Inc.

Chapter 2: God of the Valleys

1. OT: 7291, James Strong, *Biblesoft's New Exhaustive Strong's Numbers and Concordance of the Bible with Expanded Greek-Hebrew Dictionary*. Copyright © 1994, 2003, 2006 Biblesoft, Inc. and International Bible Translators, Inc.

2. OT: 5911, James Strong, *Biblesoft's New Exhaustive Strong's Numbers and Concordance of the Bible with Expanded Greek-Hebrew Dictionary*.

Chapter 5: Specially Protected to Live Unafraid

1. OT: 1657, James Strong, *Biblesoft's New Exhaustive Strong's Numbers and Concordance of the Bible with Expanded Greek-Hebrew Dictionary*. Copyright © 1994, 2003, 2006 Biblesoft, Inc. and International Bible Translators, Inc.

Chapter 6: The Power of Rest in a Crisis

1. OT: 7965, James Strong, *Biblesoft's New Exhaustive Strong's Numbers and Concordance of the Bible with Expanded Greek-Hebrew Dictionary*. Copyright © 1994, 2003, 2006 Biblesoft, Inc. and International Bible Translators, Inc.

2. "Crisis," Merriam-Webster, accessed May 11, 2020, https://www.merriam-webster.com/dictionary/crisis.

3. OT: 3427, James Strong, *Biblesoft's New Exhaustive Strong's Numbers and Concordance of the Bible with Expanded Greek-Hebrew Dictionary.*

4. OT: 3898, Joseph Henry Thayer, Francis Brown, Samuel Rolles Driver, and Charles Augustus Briggs, *The Online Bible Thayer's Greek Lexicon and Brown, Driver & Briggs Hebrew Lexicon*. Copyright © 1993, Woodside Bible Fellowship, Ontario, Canada. Licensed from the Institute for Creation Research.

5. OT: 3899, James Strong, *Biblesoft's New Exhaustive Strong's Numbers and Concordance of the Bible with Expanded Greek-Hebrew Dictionary.*

SPECIAL APPRECIATION

Special thanks and appreciation to all who have sent in their testimonies and praise reports to us. Kindly note that all testimonies are received in good faith and have been shared only with the consent of the testimony writers. Each testimony has been edited only for brevity and fluency. Names have been changed to protect the writers' privacy.

MEDICAL DISCLAIMER

If you are facing a physical or mental health condition, please understand that this book is not meant to take the place of professional medical advice. If you or your loved one has a health concern or an existing medical condition, please do consult a qualified medical practitioner or healthcare provider. We would also advise you to ask and seek the Lord always for His wisdom and guidance regarding your specific health or medical issue, and to exercise godly wisdom in the management of your own physical, mental, and emotional well-being. Do not, on your own accord, disregard any professional medical advice or diagnosis. Please also do not take what has been shared in this book as permission or encouragement to stop taking your medication or going for medical treatment. While we make no guarantees and recognize that different individuals experience different results, we continue to stand in faith to believe and affirm God's Word and healing promises with all who believe.

EXTRA RESOURCES

To hear Joseph Prince preach on the biblical principles and truths shared in each chapter of this book, please check out the following messages at JosephPrince.com/sermons.

Chapter 1: Hope That Doesn't Disappoint

Why You Can Expect Good Things to Happen to You (May 29, 2005)

Chapter 2: God of the Valleys

Present Help in Times of Trouble (September 1, 2019)

Answers for Dark Nights and Difficult Seasons (August 18, 2019)

Win the Battle over Hopelessness (August 25, 2019)

Chapter 3: Last to First When You Trust His Goodness

Last to First When You Trust His Goodness (July 15, 2018)

Chapter 4: Change How You See, Change Your Life

Change How You See and Change Your Life (December 3, 2017)

Chapter 5: Specially Protected to Live Unafraid

The Promise of Protection—Truths from Psalm 91 (July 20, 2014)

Intimacy with the Father Brings Protection—Truths from Psalm 91 (July 27, 2014)

Protection from Danger, Accidents and Disease—Truths from Psalm 91 (August 3, 2014)

Chapter 6: The Power of Rest in a Crisis

Fear Not! Christ Is in the Crisis (March 22, 2020)

Chapter 7: Expect to Receive God's Much-More Restoration

The Year of His Restoration (January 4, 2015)

Restoration for Your Losses (January 11, 2015)

Chapter 8: The King Who Came to Serve

Know Him Whose Heart Is to Serve You (March 12, 2017)

SALVATION PRAYER

If you would like to receive all that Jesus has done for you and make Him your Lord and Savior, please pray this prayer:

Lord Jesus, thank You for loving me and dying for me on the cross. Your precious blood washes me clean of every sin. You are my Lord and my Savior, now and forever. I believe You rose from the dead and that You are alive today. Because of Your finished work, I am now a beloved child of God and heaven is my home. Thank You for giving me eternal life and filling my heart with Your peace and joy. Amen.

WE WOULD LIKE TO HEAR FROM YOU

If you have prayed the salvation prayer or if you have a testimony to share after reading this book, please tell us about it via JosephPrince.com/testimony.

STAY CONNECTED WITH JOSEPH

Connect with Joseph through these social media channels and receive daily inspirational teachings:

Facebook.com/JosephPrince

Twitter.com/JosephPrince

Youtube.com/JosephPrinceOnline

Instagram: @JosephPrince

FREE DAILY E-MAIL DEVOTIONAL

Sign up for Joseph's free daily e-mail devotional at JosephPrince.com/meditate and receive bite-size inspirations to help you grow in grace.

BOOKS BY JOSEPH PRINCE

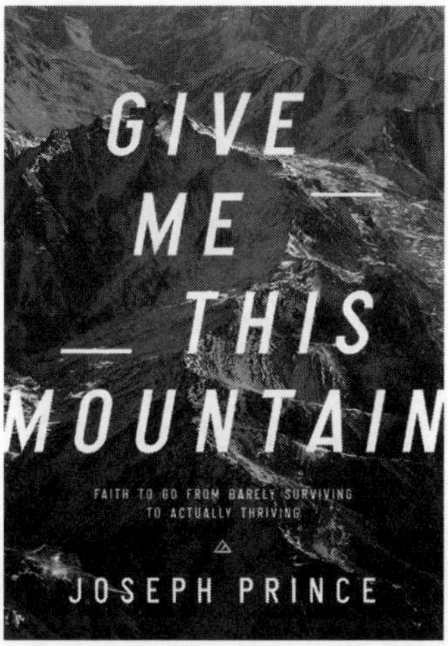

Give Me This Mountain—Faith to Go from Barely Surviving to Actually Thriving

Ever feel like life is an uphill battle that can't be won? In *Give Me This Mountain*, follow the story of a man in the Bible called Caleb, who ran headfirst into a literal uphill battle against fierce enemy forces because he held on to God's promise of victory. Over four weeks, discover powerful and relevant truths about faith, resilience, and hope, and engage with thought-provoking reflection questions and activities that will help you apply these keys in your own life. This young adult resource will inspire you to conquer every mountain of adversity and possess God's best for your life!

Unstoppable Faith

Unstoppable Faith—31 Thoughts for Owning Your Portion brings you simple yet powerful thoughts on faith, one for each day of the month. Each thought in this pocket-size resource is accompanied by an encouraging scripture and bite-size devotional reading that will help you take small steps of faith daily. When you're feeling low on faith, this book will turn your eyes away from yourself and fix them on Jesus and His grace. Beautifully designed and filled with inspirational images, *Unstoppable Faith* will help you bask in the Lord's love for you as you trust Him for the turnarounds you need in your life.

Unmerited Favor

Begin to live out the dreams God has birthed in your heart! *Unmerited Favor* builds on foundational truths of God's grace and takes you into a deeper understanding of the gift of righteousness that you have through the cross and how it gives you a supernatural ability to succeed in life. Packed with empowering new covenant truths, this book will set you free to soar above your challenges and lead an overcoming life as God's beloved today.

ABOUT THE AUTHOR

JOSEPH PRINCE is a leading voice in proclaiming the gospel of grace to a whole new generation of believers and leaders. He is the senior pastor of New Creation Church in Singapore, a vibrant and dynamic church with a congregation of more than 33,000 attendees. He separately heads Joseph Prince Ministries, a television and media broadcast ministry that is reaching the world with the good news about the Lord Jesus' finished work. Joseph is also the bestselling author of *The Power of Right Believing* and *Destined to Reign* and a highly sought-after conference speaker. For more information about his other inspiring resources and his latest audio and video messages, visit JosephPrince.com.